"Shelley Quinn's new book will be an encouragement to you in the greatest love relationship of your life. What she has done is significant. It will be a blessing and an inspiration to you in deepening your beautiful ties with Jesus."

Ruthie Jacobsen
Director, General Conference Prayer Ministries

"*Pressing in to His Presence* will enrich your life and inspire you to spend more time with Jesus. It speaks directly to the heart in practical terms and answers important questions about how to pray. This is one of the best books I have read on the science of prayer. It gave me the help I needed in making my prayer life richer. I highly recommend it to anyone who desires a closer relationship with God."

Kenneth Cox
evangelist and author

"*Pressing in to His Presence* is simultaneously an intimate walk through God's sanctuary and Shelley's own journey. It is saturated in Scripture and, more importantly, in sound scriptural reasoning. The sequential PRAISE structure for prayer is well-developed but not overly formulaic. *Pressing in to His Presence* will, I am confident, bring lasting benefit and blessing to those who read and apply its words."

David Asscherick
Director, ARISE

Pressing in to HIS PRESENCE

3ABN BOOKS

P.O. Box 220
West Frankfort, IL 62896

Pacific Press® Publishing Association
Nampa, Idaho
Oshawa, Ontario, Canada
www.pacificpress.com

Cover design by Christique Neibauer cqgraphicdesign.com
Cover image by Shutterstock.com
Back cover photo by Kenton Rogers
Inside design by Aaron Troia

Additional copies of this book are available from two locations:

3ABN: Call 1-800-752-3226 or visit www.3ABN.org.

Adventist Book Centers: Call 1-800-765-6855 or visit www.adventistbookcenter.com.

3ABN Books is dedicated to bringing you the best in published materials consistent with the mission of Three Angels Broadcasting Network. Our goal is to uplift Jesus through books, audio, and video materials by our family of 3ABN presenters. Our in-depth Bible study guides, devotionals, biographies, and lifestyle materials promote the whole person in health and the mending of broken people. For more information, call 616-627-4651 or visit 3ABN's Web site: www.3ABN.org.

Library of Congress Cataloging-in-Publication Data:

Quinn, Shelley (Shelley J.), 1949-
  Pressing in to His presence : developing an intimate relationship with
Christ through prayer / Shelley Quinn.
     p. cm.
  ISBN 13: 978-0-8163-2412-5 (pbk.)
  ISBN 10: 0-8163-2412-3 (pbk.)
  1. Prayer—Christianity. 2. Spiritual life—Christianity. I. Title.
  BV210.3.Q46 2010
  248.3'2—dc22

                                                                2010009436

10 11 12 13 14 • 5 4 3 2 1

DEDICATION

This book is dedicated to those who desire to experience the loving embrace of the Lord's fellowship. Just as it has done for me, I pray this teaching will bring *you* into closer communion with the One who knows you intimately and loves you despite your imperfections.

May the Holy Spirit ignite in your heart a flame of passion for God's presence, convincing you that prayer is the greatest pursuit of the day!

"Let us therefore come boldly to the throne of grace, that we may obtain mercy and find grace to help in time of need" *(Hebrews 4:16)*.

Contents

A Passion for His Presence

CHAPTER 1

For most of my adult life, I've resided in rural areas—out-of-the-way places that required driving forlorn stretches of highway to reach cities of significant population. Access to shopping or the nearest major airport has always been a hassle. Still, any inconvenience of the time-consuming travel has been offset by treasured times of talking with God in one of my favorite "prayer closets"—my car.

Jesus said, "Enter into thy closet, and when thou hast shut thy door, pray to thy Father" *(Matthew 6:6, KJV)*. Perhaps He wasn't thinking of driving seventy miles per hour down the highway while praying, and He probably wouldn't recommend total absorption in prayer while surrounded by heavy traffic, but my only traffic concerns were avoiding the occasional tumbleweed or the absentminded jackrabbit ambling across the path of my prayer-closet-on-wheels.

I'll never forget the evening I headed west from our farm in Coleman, Texas, to visit my sister in New Mexico. Slinging my suitcase into the back of the car, I plopped down in the driver's seat and pulled the door closed—shutting the world out. Eagerly anticipating the seven-hour trip before me, I prayed and headed down the road.

No radio or CDs for me! With precious little time to myself, driving miles of nearly empty highways was something to be relished. The undisturbed silence served as an incubator for my inner thoughts. Soon, like bubbles of oxygen escaping the depth of murky waters, they began to surface. I'm often surprised, even amused, by some of these "bubble thoughts."

The roadways were lighted by a full moon. Only an occasional set of oncoming headlights interrupted the serenity of the landscape. Once I reached the interstate, there would be just thirty miles to navigate before returning to less-traveled, even desolate, roads for the rest of the journey. Ahead was another adventure with only my favorite Companion—the Lord. Little did I know what God had in store for me!

I have previously shared the story you are about to read with only two people. They both seem startled. Opening my heart like this is risky business—I chance being misunderstood and labeled "strange." Let me emphasize, it was a one-time occurrence in my life. This particular experience is *not* what the teaching of this book is about. It is, however, related in an exotic kind of way, so—I'll risk telling you.

First, let me ask you a question.

Have you ever prayed for more than six hours without distraction or interruption? It has been my privilege only once—on that moonlit night in 1996. It was an extraordinary event that began with a scripture I was affirming.

> Hear, O LORD, when I cry with my voice!
> Have mercy also upon me, and answer me.
> When You said, "Seek My face,"
> My heart said to You, "Your face, LORD, I will seek."
> Do not hide Your face from me;
> Do not turn Your servant away in anger;
> You have been my help;
> Do not leave me nor forsake me,
> O God of my salvation
> *(Psalm 27:7–9).*

Spoken aloud, these words shattered the silence and startled me with their intensity. I wasn't merely quoting Scripture. Rather, this was a sincere heart cry. For more than a week, the clamor of constant distractions had eclipsed my time of worship with the Lord. A deep sense of loss now overshadowed me—I mourned the lack of intimate fellowship with the Lover of my soul.

Deep calls unto "deep"

As I began thanking God for His countless blessings, praise for His goodness and mercy welled in my heart and flowed from my lips. I pleaded for forgiveness as I confessed the many ways in which I had failed Him. Soon I was praying Scripture promises—returning God's Word to Him with thanksgiving—fully persuaded He had the power to perform what He had promised.[1] It was as if I inhaled relief and life, and exhaled every negative feeling that numbed my joy.

Striving to worship in truth and in spirit,[2] I longed to draw nearer to Him—to "press in" to His presence. He was definitely drawing nearer to me.[3]

I jokingly tell you the car was on autopilot that night. Those frequently traveled roadways were so familiar. This journey required no concentration on directions, which freed me to become completely immersed in worship of my Lord and Savior. Six hours of seeking His face were swiftly absorbed in the spongelike draw of this bliss.

A familiar landmark appeared, announcing that only forty-five miles remained to my destination.

"Oh, I'm not ready to stop worshiping, Lord! I've never before sensed Your presence so richly! It's true, Father, 'In Your presence is fullness of joy; at Your right hand are pleasures forevermore.'[4] I love You, Lord, with all my heart, soul, and mind. Cause me to love You with all of my strength![5] 'As the deer pants for the water brooks, so pants my soul for You, O God.' "[6]

What happened next is *indescribable*. My attempt to explain it will be feeble, at best. It was an Acts 2 upper room–type of experience—not with a mighty rushing wind and tongues of fire, but certainly with an *outpouring* of His Spirit.

Suddenly, unexpectedly—as cymbals striking together in a symphonic crescendo—ecstatic joy cascaded over me in wave after wave! Words are insufficient to describe it. It was the type of experience that you might expect Handel's "Hallelujah Chorus" to accompany, but it didn't. I sensed God was communicating with me, but not in any language. It was *Deep calling unto deep—His heart calling unto my heart, His Spirit calling unto my spirit.* He flooded me with His love!

> Deep calls unto deep at the noise of Your waterfalls;
> All Your waves and billows have gone over me.
> The LORD will command His lovingkindness in the daytime,
> And in the night His song shall be with me—
> A prayer to the God of my life
> *(Psalm 42:7, 8).*

Pressing in to His Presence

If there is one thing Bible commentators agree on, it is that King David was pouring out emotions of devastation as he penned Psalm 42. Cut off from worshiping in the sanctuary, David was distressed with holy zeal for God. His soul thirsted for living water from the living Lord! Most commentators believe David refers, in verse 7, to the overwhelming afflictions of his soul as being God's "waves and billows" cascading over him.

I'm not a theologian, and don't presume to correct Bible commentators. Still, after my experience of pressing in to His presence that night, I can't help but look at Psalm 42 through a different lens.

David wrote, "Why are you in despair, O my soul? And why have you become disturbed within me? Hope in God, for I shall again praise Him for the help of His presence" *(Psalm 42:5, NASB)*.

Is it possible that in the midst of his angst, David pressed in to God's presence and experienced the same unique visitation I had? Is that why he was able to rise so rapidly from the depths of despondency to the heights of faith and confidence?

The apostle John wrote, "I heard a voice from heaven, like the voice of many waters" *(Revelation 14:2)*. When David referred to "the noise" of God's waterfalls, was he describing God's presence pouring out over him in powerful *wordless* communication—Deep calling unto deep—like the voice of many waters?

Could that explain what he wrote in the next verse, "The LORD will command His lovingkindness in the daytime, and in the night His song shall be with me—a prayer to the God of my life" *(Psalm 42:8)*, and why he concluded with these words: "Why are you cast down, O my soul? And why are you disquieted within me? Hope in God; for I shall yet praise Him, the help of my countenance and my God" *(verse 11)*?

I don't mean to take poetic license or try to rewrite Bible commentary. This is simply something that causes me to wonder. Because it is not a doctrinal matter, I trust it is okay to share my musings about David's experience in relation to my own.

Sadly, this encounter was a one-time occurrence in my life. Never since have I communed with God for six hours in such earnest, uninterrupted prayer. Oh, yes, I've attended all-night prayer vigils where we prayed around the clock. Still, these were times of seeking God's hand to move in specific answers to prayer—not an uninterrupted season of sincerely seeking His face.

I chide myself, sometimes, for being spiritually lazy and apathetic. Why haven't I tried to repeat the unique events of that evening? I'm afraid it wouldn't happen again if I were to seek "the experience." It would be difficult to duplicate the intensity of that night. If I go to God with the expectation of some type of phenomenal experience, I am seeking Him for the wrong reason and in danger of receiving a psychologically induced result. So, I will settle for this perhaps once-in-a-lifetime event.

You may doubt what I have just shared, attributing the event to emotionalism. That's okay. I confess that hearing such a story from someone else would leave me skeptical. My defense is simply that I am not an overly emotional person— nor am I a sensationalist. This story was told *not* to tout the tale of a mountaintop experience, but merely to illustrate the power of heartfelt prayer.

Prayer is like a multifaceted diamond—the benefits of prayer are likewise multifaceted. Our practice of prayer needs a little polishing to realize its brilliance. We too often regard the purpose of prayer as the matter of simply laying our requests before God. Ah, but it's so much more! The underlying purpose of prayer is to *know God* on a more intimate level, *by communicating with Him* on a more intimate level.

Developing the passion

> "For I know the plans I have for you," declares the LORD, "plans
> to prosper you and not to harm you, plans to give you hope and a future.
> *Then* you will call upon me and come and pray to me, and I will listen to you.
> You will seek me and find me when you seek me with all your heart. I will be
> found by you," declares the LORD, "and will bring you back from captivity"
> (*Jeremiah 29:11–14, NIV; emphasis added*).

Look at the previous verses again and note the emphasis I've added to the word *then*.

The question is *when*? When do we call upon God, seeking Him with all of our hearts?

I recall when I first pondered this passage. The sentences seemed out of order. Should they not have been arranged in the reverse, listing first the call for our wholehearted search for God? *Then,* after we sought Him, He would answer and explain that He was the One with a plan for our confused lives.

"What are you trying to tell us, Lord?" I asked.

"When you recognize I have a good plan for your life, then *you will be motivated to seek me with all of your heart,"* He answered in that still, small, *inaudible* voice.[7]

God has a plan for our lives, and it's better than the one we are living! We find it in His Holy Word. As we discover His plan, acknowledge His sovereignty and power, and understand He performs on behalf of our eternal benefit ("according to the purpose of Him who works all things according to the counsel of His will," *Ephesians 1:11*), our hearts well up with eager expectation. We develop an incredible desire to spend time in the counsel of His will—the Bible. We exert increased effort to a wholehearted communication with the Lover of our souls.

In other words, we develop a passion for His presence!

A greater understanding of God's plan for our lives naturally progresses to a passion for His presence. The closer we draw near to Him, the more we grow to be like Him. As we become more Christlike, we develop increased sensitivity to His moment-by-moment presence. He is with us always—He never leaves us or forsakes us.[8]

If we're not experiencing His presence, it is due to our indifference. Spiritual indifference is a dangerous heart condition.

King David had a passion for God's presence. That passion caused him to seek God earnestly. In return, God sought David—sought him to be king, calling him "a man after His own heart" *(1 Samuel 13:14).*

In his prayer journal, David—referring to himself—wrote these words to God, "For You have made him [David] most blessed forever; You have made him exceedingly glad with Your presence" *(Psalm 21:6).*

We can look to the Old Testament and realize that David's spiritual life had its ebbs and flows. Still, his desire for God's presence always returned as consuming waves of passion. In the wilderness of Judah, David wrote these words:

> O God, you are my God,
> earnestly I seek you;
> my soul thirsts for you,
> my body longs for you,
> in a dry and weary land

> where there is no water.
> I have seen you in the sanctuary
> and beheld your power and your glory.
> Because your love is better than life,
> my lips will glorify you.
> I will praise you as long as I live,
> and in your name I will lift up my hands
> *(Psalm 63:1–4, NIV)*.

Do you desire to be like David? To be God's loving child, seeking Him earnestly—a person after His own heart? To experience the reward God has for those who earnestly seek Him?[9] Oh, I do! Unfortunately, as with David's occasional omission, I, too, experience an ebb tide of my passion for His presence. It makes me wonder why the tides have turned and are outgoing.

I see a parallel with the moon. There are times when the moon fully reflects the sun's glory on earth, while at other times its position to the sun causes it to appear dark. It is the moon on the move, not the sun. Both conditions affect the rhythmic ebb and flow of ocean tides on our rotating planet.

As the moon reflects the sunlight, so I reflect the glory of God's Son at the times when I am turned full-faced toward Him. Unfortunately, sometimes my position to the Son veils His reflection in my life. It is I who moves, not the Son. Both conditions affect the degree of my passion for His presence.

Have you ever lost the rhythm of your relationship with God? Have you ever just awakened one morning and wondered what happened to your zeal for prayer and Bible study? The cares of this world can be like crashing waves that wash the best of our intentions out to sea.

I can't fully explain these cyclic rises and falls in my spinning-earth life. Why do I occasionally turn my face from Him? Oh, I believe I am still headed in His direction and that I remain His child, but it hurts me to disappoint my loving Father. Praise God, the reverse flows are short lived. My passion for God's presence always returns again like a surging tidal wave washing over me!

Watch and pray

It was September 1999. For the previous eighteen months, I had traveled the

United States, working twelve-hour days, six to seven days a week with a start-up company in Houston, Texas. A hectic travel schedule made it impossible to attend my Sunday keeping church.

I reasoned this was a special career opportunity and promised God it would be only for a limited time that I forsook the assembling of His saints,[10] as well as the practice of speaking and praying life affirmations from Scripture (explained in chapter 6). I dutifully read a chapter of the Bible each night, hoping it would suffice. Lots of Scripture was hidden in my heart—I felt secure.

Unwittingly, I had unplugged from my power Source. Operating on spiritual battery power as my standby, I failed to notice how badly I needed a recharge. In fact, I had not yet recognized the spiritual energy generated by speaking God's Scripture promises over my life and returning them to Him in prayer.

Over those many months, my prayer life had gradually diminished to several minutes here and there during the day, and the obligatory prayer at meals and bedtime (little prayers are often just salve for the conscience). The Scripture I had hidden in my heart was playing out.

God's promises no longer sparked my thoughts without effort. I had been unplugged too long from the spiritually life-affirming power source of speaking God's promises over my life. My spiritual current was rapidly discharging.

I lamented my loss of intimacy with the Lord. I'm embarrassed to admit my prayers became increasingly whiny as I begged God to change me, while making no sincere effort to change my own behavior.

Once again faulty reasoning caused me to assign higher priority to my job than to seeking God's kingdom first.[11] I thought I had a good excuse. My husband, J.D., had joined me twelve months earlier in becoming employed by the same start-up company that demanded such personal sacrifice. Like a NASA shuttle, the trajectory of their success had skyrocketed. Then the unthinkable happened. They filed for bankruptcy, owing us a good deal of money we knew we could never collect.

J.D. took temporary work in the panhandle of Texas, while I scrambled to take advantage of a business opportunity of our own. To meet the mid-January launch deadline of our new company, I worked twelve to fourteen hours a day from home developing business-building seminars for clients of CPAs. Giving God more empty promises, my days were consumed with work, and my nights with pouty prayers.

It was glaringly obvious I had lost my sense of peace and desperately needed rest—rest in the Lord. My spiritual apathy grieved God. I had forfeited the favor of intimate fellowship with Him.

Moses' pleading for the Lord's presence came to mind. He had prayed for God to grant him—and the erring people of Israel—the return of His presence to accompany them as they made their way to the promised Land.

Our God of infinite love replied, "My Presence will go with you, and I will give you rest" *(Exodus 33:14)*.

That's what I needed—His presence and His rest!

Walking outside into the crisp night air that evening, I gazed at His celestial glory. The spectacle of the starry host blurred, as hot, stinging tears brimmed in my eyes.

"Father, please forgive me for forsaking my First Love!"[12]

That was all I said, but it was *not* all that the Lord heard. When troubled eyes are turned toward heaven, the tender trickle of tears is heard by our loving Father as *prayer*.

"He does not forget the cry of the humble" *(Psalm 9:12)*.

Misplaced priorities and negligence in prayer testified to a life that was not fully surrendered to the Lord. I was humbled. It was time for a change, and change was in the wind. The direction of the tides was turning. My passion for His presence surged!

---

1. Romans 4:21.
2. John 4:23.
3. James 4:8.
4. Psalm 16:11.
5. Mark 12:30.
6. Psalm 42:1.
7. 1 Kings 19:12.
8. Hebrews 13:5.
9. Hebrews 11:6.
10. Hebrews 10:25.
11. Matthew 6:33.
12. Revelation 2:4.

Raising My "Ebenezer"

CHAPTER 2

Does this sound at all familiar? Your priorities are out of order—you know you are slighting God—and a fog of frustration has settled in. Finally, remorse leads you down one of two paths. Either, burdened with guilt, you begin avoiding God (spending even less time seeking His presence), or, in your turmoil, you cry out to Him for an explanation of why you are so prone to wander from the One you love.

Perhaps, as I have experienced in my past, instead of standing firm as a spiritual warrior, you find that you have become a weak-kneed spiritual whiner.

There is some comfort—but very little—in knowing that our condition is not all that uncommon. It's rather like being diagnosed with cancer, but told not to worry because many are likewise afflicted. Here is the good news: God will provide a way out when we become serious about seeking Him. Consider the words of this old hymn, "Come, Thou Fount of Every Blessing."

Come, Thou Fount of every blessing,
Tune my heart to sing Thy grace;
Streams of mercy, never ceasing,
Call for songs of loudest praise.
Teach me some melodious sonnet,
Sung by flaming tongues above;
Praise the mount! I'm fixed upon it,
Mount of Thy redeeming love....

Here I raise my Ebenezer;
Here by Thy great help I've come;
And I hope, by Thy good pleasure,
Safely to arrive at home.

Jesus sought me when a stranger,
Wandering from the fold of God;
He, to rescue me from danger,
Interposed His precious blood; …

O to grace how great a debtor
Daily I'm constrained to be!
Let Thy goodness, like a fetter,
Bind my wandering heart to Thee.
Prone to wander, Lord, I feel it,
Prone to leave the God I love;
Here's my heart, O take and seal it,
Seal it for Thy courts above.

Doesn't that sentiment cause comfort to calm your heart? We are not the only ones in this boat riding a sea of troubled waters. There is hope for us, after all! There is God!

After singing this hymn recently in church, a sweet little lady sitting next to me whispered, "What's an Ebenezer?" I explained it meant "stone of help" and refers back to the prophet Samuel erecting a monument for God's divine assistance in battle: "Then Samuel took a stone and set it between Mizpah and Shen, and he called the name of it Ebenezer [stone of help], saying, Heretofore the Lord has helped us" *(1 Samuel 7:12, AMP).*

In my personal spiritual battle, God intervened in an interesting way. The teaching I share in this book is how the Lord led me out of a backslidden condition and gave me victory over the enemy. This teaching has been my Ebenezer since 1999. I have shared it around the world. By experience, I can tell you it contains the power of God to prevent backsliding.

On the road again

God grabbed my attention that September of 1999 as I made my monthly grocery shopping trek of sixty miles from my country home to the nearest Sam's Club (a retail outlet that sells in bulk quantities). This breakthrough also came to me in the prayer-closet of my car. Shutting out all the distractions of our new business and the world, I began praying to understand my backsliding.

"Lord, I don't understand it. You know I love You. How can I walk so closely that at times I sense Your heartbeat, and then plunge to such a backslidden condition? Please, Lord, explain why this happens to me!"

My pleadings were earnest for that hour, but I reached my destination with no answer to my dilemma. I made an agreement with the Lord to continue the prayer after my shopping was completed. This was one day I didn't dawdle in Sam's Club. I was a woman on a mission—eager to get back to God. I checked out at the register, tossed my purchased items in the back of the vehicle, jumped in, and buckled up for the ride.

By the time the car was in gear, I was again pleading with the Lord for a solution to my problem. Praying aloud for the next thirty miles, my tone became less whiny and more insistent on understanding what I should do.

"Please, Lord, show me the way out of this pit, and teach me how I can prevent this from happening again!"

Suddenly, the still, small voice of the Lord whispered to my heart. This is the Voice spoken of in 1 Kings 19:12, which I have come to believe represents times when the Holy Spirit impresses God's thoughts on our minds with inaudible words.

"Child, if you will come to Me and spend an hour in prayer each morning, I promise you will never backslide again."

What? Flabbergasted, I did not respond to Him. My mind was churning. *An hour a day in prayer? Who could keep that up?* Well, of course, that would keep anyone from backsliding. Even if we lost ground during the day, we would be starting over again the next morning. His mercies are new every morning.[1] If we began each day by spending an hour with God, how could we stay backslidden? *If only I could practice this advice, it would be impossible to lose touch with Him. Who am I kidding? I couldn't do that!*

"But, Lord," I protested loudly, "You know I'm not that disciplined! My life is so manic—there are too many demands on my time. I can't promise You I'll spend an hour in prayer each morning. Father God, I'm not disciplined enough to make that commitment to You. Lord, it would have to be *You* empowering me to do that and . . ."

My voice trailed off as the clear truth of that last statement arrested my attention. *Of course, it would have to be God's prompting and God's enabling to help me keep such an overwhelming commitment!* Teenagers in the United States have a rude saying when someone states the obvious, "Well, duh!" Duh, indeed. I had voiced what God knew already. He was just waiting for me to recognize how much I needed His help.

Jesus said, "I am the vine, you are the branches. He who abides in Me, and I in him, bears much fruit; for without Me you can do nothing" *(John 15:5)*. He also promised that His grace is sufficient for us, and that His power is made perfect in our weakness.[2]

The remaining miles home were driven in astonished silence. I was wrestling, not with God, but with my own dazed thoughts. There had been many occasions in my life when I had prayed for an hour. But every day? *How can I consistently practice that? I'm always on the run, too busy for my own good. What would I say to Him every day for an hour? Won't my prayers become repetitious?*

The words of Deuteronomy 30:19, 20, streamed through my mind. *"I have set before you life and death, blessing and cursing; therefore choose life, that . . . you . . . may live; that you may love the LORD your God, that you may obey His voice, and that you may cling to Him, for He is your life and the length of your days."*

This was a familiar voice, speaking familiar words—I knew it was from God. In 1995, He had set before me another spiritual life-and-death choice when He called me into a more intimate relationship with His Word. God had explained how His Word was life to me, and that if I chose to cling to His promises, I was choosing life. I made the right choice then. Now, it was time to make another.

God did not command me to pray an hour each morning. That isn't one of His requirements for salvation. Maybe I was in greater spiritual jeopardy than I realized. It was as if I had fallen overboard again, and He was throwing a new lifeline to His child who was in danger of going down for the third time.

Pressing in to His Presence

It was up to me to choose whether I grabbed hold or not. He had set before me another life-and-death decision, so to speak, and I wanted to choose His abundant life.

I was weary of my spiritual stupor. My spirit was willing, but my weak flesh trembled. I didn't want to disappoint Him as the disciples had in the Garden of Gethsemane, when Christ's inner circle (Peter, James, and John) demonstrated so little commitment in watching and praying with Him for an hour.

> Then He came to the disciples and found them sleeping,
> and said to Peter, "What! You could not watch with Me
> one hour? Watch and pray, lest you enter into temptation.
> The spirit indeed is willing, but the flesh is weak"
> *(Matthew 26:40, 41).*

Reaching home, I parked the car and sat in stunned silence for a few moments. Finally, a whisper escaped my lips, "OK, Father. I will make a commitment to pray one hour each day—it's not a promise, but I will commit to cooperate with You. Of course, Lord, I'm relying on Your help. You will have to motivate me. You will have to teach me how to pray every day for an hour. We'll start first thing tomorrow morning."

Write the vision and make it plain

The next morning, I rose at my usual hour of 5:00 A.M. It seemed wise to eat breakfast first—that would surely increase my concentration power for the upcoming hour. Naturally, I watched the morning news during breakfast, as was my habit. Being an obsessive housekeeper, I washed dishes, tidied the kitchen, took out the trash, and made the bed before praying. That would purge those pesky distractions. Soon, I opted to shower and dress before meeting with the Lord, reasoning it would make me a more bright-eyed and bushy-tailed disciple (unlike Peter, James, and John).

In the shower, the fact of the matter washed over me. My old familiar pattern of procrastination had surfaced. Ashamed, I determined to quickly ready myself and to keep my appointment with God without further delay.

Grabbing my Bible, I descended the stairs to the family room and chose a comfy chair for our meeting spot (my back would not endure an hour on my knees). Clasping my hands and bowing my head, I inquired of the Lord how to begin. Suddenly, I was strongly impressed to journal my prayer—to write it out as a love letter to God.

I had never written a prayer before, but thought about the Psalms. Isn't that what they are—the written prayers of David (and a few others) that were later set to music? Was it God impressing me to do this, or did this thought originate from me?

Glancing at the open Bible on my lap, my eyes fell on Habakkuk 2:2, 3: "Then the LORD answered me and said: 'Write the vision and make it plain on tablets, that he may run who reads it. For the vision is yet for an appointed time; but at the end it will speak, and it will not lie. Though it tarries, wait for it; because it will surely come, it will not tarry.' "

That was a sufficient answer for me. But, handwritten prayer presented a problem. I think much faster than I write. When I'm writing hurriedly, my penmanship can rival any physician's chicken-scratch handwriting. I've often tried to decipher my own notes scribbled in haste—it's much like trying to decode hieroglyphics.

Before we continue, I need to add a disclaimer here—journaling is not for everyone. It isn't required to journal your prayers to follow the teaching of this book. My husband, J.D., is a mighty man of prayer. If someone told J.D. that he must write his prayer to "press in" to God's presence, I doubt he would ever try. Another precious saint who experimented with journaling reported that it seemed to diminish the intimacy of her prayers. I quickly exclaimed, "Then don't do it!"

Still, I encourage everyone to try it at least once. For many people, journaling increases focus—and increased focus results in increased intimacy. What do I mean?

Have you ever been on your knees, praying to the God you love, while in midstream of a sentence, and your mind wanders? *I must remember to pick up the dry cleaning.* Ashamed, you apologize to God, only to find your mind wandering again. *I forgot to return David's call last night; I hope it wasn't urgent! Oh, Lord, forgive me; I don't mean to get off track.* With added urgency you purpose to focus on what you are praying. Abruptly, another wayward thought interrupts. *Is my doctor's appointment this afternoon? Who will pick the children up from school?* You sigh, throw a leash around that thought, and direct your mind to God once again.

It would surprise me if you have never suffered this common prayer-time trend. Our minds *are* prone to wander. Keeping our thoughts confined is like trying to keep puppies in a box.

Journaling is a more deliberate activity than merely thinking, and it engages more of your senses. It involves writing and consequently seeing your meditations on paper. The more of your senses engaged, the greater your focus. And, *the greater the focus, the greater the intimacy of prayer.*

At 3ABN's 2009 spring camp meeting, I presented an abbreviated version of this teaching. My pastor, John Lomacang, dropped by my office several days later to say he had tried journaling for the first time. Delighted by the increased prayer dynamics, he shared his intentions to continue writing his prayers.

On with my story—I'm a fast typist, so I asked the Lord if typing my prayer at the computer was acceptable. How do you think He responded? Does it seem like something God would frown upon—spending an hour at the computer, writing Him a love letter?

I bolted upstairs to my office, opened a new Word file on my computer, typed the date at the top of the page, and glanced at the clock to confirm the time. It was already 8:00 A.M., and I had a lot to accomplish that day. I didn't want the temptation of checking the clock every ten minutes for the next hour, so I stuck a sticky-note sheet over the clock's face.

"Father, please teach me how to pray. How do You want me to pray the next hour? I need Your help!"

The following chapters will take you through what I learned from the Lord that day (and in the weeks ahead). God taught me how to "press in" to His presence in such a way that the practice could be sustained daily with joy.

I've never been a fan of prayer "formulas"—there is always the possibility of developing a mechanical and meaningless practice. I don't think of this teaching as a prayer formula, but rather as prayer "portions" or a prayer "pattern." In over ten years of practicing this type of prayer, it has never become mechanical for me.

Two-way communication

At the Lord's leading, the prayer developed that morning in the following order: praise was the opening segment, followed by repentance, intercession, and supplication. I finished pouring out my heart to God and couldn't think of another thing to pray.

How much longer did I have to go before my hour was complete? What else was there to talk about at this moment?

Thinking perhaps forty-five minutes had passed, I peeked under the sticky-note on the clock to check the time. It was already a quarter past ten. I had spent two hours and fifteen minutes with the Lord. Amazing! As I typed the words "In Jesus' name, Amen!" that still, small voice of the Lord interrupted, catching me totally off guard.

"Be still, and know that I am God!"

I know the Holy Spirit will never impress anything upon our minds that is not in perfect agreement with God's counsel in the Bible. Those words were a direct quote of Psalm 46:10. I froze in position with my fingers poised on the keyboard.

Then I began to doubt, *Was that really God's command to be still, or was it my imagination?* Another distant thought came drifting into my mind.

"Oh, Lord, is this You, or is this me?" I frantically queried.

Yet another thought, and again I questioned the source, "Lord, please, is this You, or is this me?"

"I will teach you to quit interrupting in the spiritual realm as well as in the physical realm. Write what I speak to you that you may take note of it often."

With trepidation I typed out the thoughts being so strongly impressed upon my mind. They amounted to three sentences and ended with the command, "Look it up!"

Searching the Bible, I found Scripture that supported and explained what I now believed were His divine thoughts, and sat back in satisfaction that my loving Father had given me instruction to heed.

I didn't really expect this to happen in the same manner on the following morning. But it did! God again spoke to me. This time it was only two sentences, but they were powerful reassurance that it was His still, small voice impressing His thoughts upon my mind.

Pressing in to His Presence

J.D. was working out of town. We regularly called each other throughout the day. Of course, I was so excited about this new prayer privilege that I had to share my joy with him! He didn't say much about it, at first. After several days of listening to my bubbling reports, he made his feelings understood.

"Honey, please don't tell anyone else that you are hearing from God," he began tenderly. "They will think you're crazy!"

Within a few weeks, J.D. was convinced God was indeed impressing thoughts upon my mind during times of prayer.

"I pray throughout the day. Why haven't I ever heard God?" he questioned.

"Well, have you ever been still and listened?"

A few days later, J.D. called and cautiously shared a new prayer experience, wondering if the thoughts that came to his mind were from God. We will examine what happened to him in chapter 11. I think you will agree with me, God was definitely giving him a loving and unexpected word of correction.

Hearing God's voice isn't an exclusive privilege offered to just a few. I'm no more special to God than anyone else. He is a loving Father, who wants to teach His children (if He could just gain their attention and cooperation to listen) that prayer is a *two-way* communication.

If this seems a little far-fetched to you, please don't put this book down yet! Please give me the opportunity to prove this is a scriptural teaching. If you don't, you won't know what you have missed!

I have polled congregations around the world, asking how many in the audience were certain that God has—on occasion, by His Holy Spirit—impressed His thoughts upon their minds in inaudible words. Almost always, at least two-thirds of the members in the audience raise their hands (some with timidity, as if they were embarrassed to admit it).

Before I learned to "press in" to His presence, those precious occasions happened to me infrequently. But it became almost a daily occurrence over the many years I faithfully practiced this teaching. Occasionally, God trusted me with His silence—to teach me He was still there, even though I didn't hear His voice.

Don't be fearful of trying this biblical practice of listening for the Lord's voice. In today's culture, we aren't accustomed to thinking God wants to communicate with us on a personal level. Oh, but He does! In chapters 10 and 11, we will examine Scripture to verify the ways the Lord communicates with humankind. We will also look at His promises that reveal God wants us to learn that prayer is a two-way communication!

I don't hear His inaudible voice when I rush in before Him and try to get an answer. In fact, it rarely happens if I haven't spent at least an hour in prayer, pouring out my heart before Him, and then sitting still before Him. When His thoughts come, they are almost always something of a very personal nature and application, and they always line up in total agreement with His Written Word!

Listening to God during my prayer time is how I knew He was calling me into full-time ministry. He also announced twenty-one months before I first appeared on 3ABN that He would open the doors for television, radio, and publishing, and that I would speak into all the world. A couple of years later, He prevented us from buying a new home in Coleman by telling us we would move out of town within seven months. He didn't reveal the location, and I didn't ask. I had already learned that God tells me just a little at a time. This was months in advance of our surprise invitation to join the staff at 3ABN.

There are times I have been in prayer with Him—feeling satisfied about myself and the direction in which I am heading—when God has stunned me with a word of correction. There have also been days when I'm crestfallen—feeling like a dismal disappointment to Him—and my loving Father has surprised me with words of encouragement and assurance. His response has never been something I have expected. I have come to trust that these thoughts being impressed upon my mind are of divine origin.

I kept my commitment to the Lord for nine years. In addition to praying throughout the day, I prayed an hour each morning. I'm ashamed to admit—but I must— that over the past year I let this practice slip. Instead of daily pressing in to His presence, it became a weekly effort, and some months it was not even that often. Working four ten-hour days each week at Three Angels Broadcasting Network and traveling most weekends to speak at camp meetings, church revivals, and retreats have interrupted the rhythm of this practice—only because I have allowed it. I'm not proud of this fact.

Don't misunderstand what I'm saying. I continue to pray often throughout the day. But, it's different. It's not "pressing in" to His presence. A fifteen-minute prayer is just not as satisfying. I don't hear from God when I rush in before Him in this fashion. And, to answer the obvious question, Yes, I lose ground when I'm not practicing this. I think that's called backsliding, isn't it?

Prior to writing this book, I felt it necessary to return to the practice of praying an hour in the morning. Praise God, He is reawakening my passion for His presence! Prayer is a vital life-source—it is the breath of the soul. How refreshing it is to be deep-breathing again, rather than the occasional spiritual gasping I had gravitated toward. More important, I cannot tell you how joyful it makes me to once again be hearing the still, small voice of the Lord!

Oh, prone to wander from the God I love—prone to take His presence for granted. Ah, to grace how great a debtor I am.

Father, take my heart and seal it. This is my prayer for all sincere-hearted seekers of Your kingdom and Your righteousness.[3]

The P-R-A-I-S-E prayer

If someone spends an hour with God each morning and learns to sit at His feet to listen, doesn't it seem plausible she could expect greater spiritual power to overcome the obstacles of sinful flesh? In my case, it just wasn't happening—at least not for the first two weeks.

On the fifteenth morning of my new prayer experience, I awoke rather late and opened the windows to the best weather September can muster. The air was crisp. Golden leaves on the ground, moist with dew, reflected the sun's sparkling rays. Normally this scene would have exhilarated me, but I was feeling down-in-the-mouth, dissatisfied with my spiritual progress.

After opening my prayer with praise, I began my ritual of repentance. Confessing my sins, I pleaded with God for more spiritual power. The still, small voice of the Lord broke through, saying, *"All of My promises are yours in Christ."*[4]

Those words struck like a thunderbolt! Of course! God had proven to me several years earlier how affirming His Word (claiming and confessing His promises; praying them back to Him) was the way to "plug in" to His power source.

I added a generous portion of life affirmations from Scripture to my daily prayer that morning. Immediately, I was transformed—"endued with power from on high."[5] The struggle of my flesh was banished. God thrust out the enemy from before me.[6]

That prayer prevailed! My day was dramatically different. Before I went to bed that night, I reviewed the prayer and decided to label the various segments—

all of the portions that had produced such a powerful pattern. These are the segment labels:

Praise
Repentance
Affirmations
Intercession
Supplication
Enter and be still *(originally "Exalt the Lord through listening")*

You will note that taking the first letter of each portion, we can derive the acronym PRAISE. I alternately refer to this teaching as "Pressing in to His presence" or "the PRAISE prayer."

I may be making too much out of this, but I wholeheartedly believe God had a reason for directing the segments in this special order. In the following chapters, you will learn why I think this is true. You can decide for yourself.

I often use this pattern in a much shorter prayer as well. Still, I'm not trying to advocate this is the only manner in which to pray. Prayer is intimate communion with an intimate Being of love and will naturally take on various forms of expression. I send up many different types of prayer daily before His throne. Still, the PRAISE prayer pattern has been the most successful I have used for pressing in to His presence.

Please don't become discouraged and put this book aside because the thought of praying an hour a day seems impossible! This is not a commandment! Our lives are so overscheduled—I really do appreciate the challenges facing you. So what if your to-do list is too demanding to accomplish this daily? You can make time on your days off from your job. At least you will be pressing in to His presence on a weekly basis. Once you have tasted the sweetness of praying this way, you very well might make time for it more often.

Martin Luther, the priest who initiated the Protestant Reformation in A.D. 1517, was known as a devout man of prayer. He reportedly said, "Tomorrow I plan to work, work from early until late. In fact, I have so much to do that I shall spend the first three hours in prayer." This testifies that Luther recognized his *absolute* dependence upon the Lord and had learned to leverage his productive time by spending precious hours with God first.

If you determine to make this appointment with God your highest priority, God will increase your productivity and make certain you accomplish everything you need to do. Speaking from experience, I can say that you will be more productive after pressing in to His presence.

May I say a prayer for you right now? I will pray according to the PRAISE pattern:

> Father, we thank You for Your love and Your grace toward us. Thank You for the indescribable gift of salvation through Jesus Christ. We praise You for Your goodness, holiness, mercy, and power. We ask, in the name of Jesus, for You to forgive our sins that we may come before You with clean hands and a pure heart. We are Your beloved sheep. We hear Your voice[7] and will follow You only, and will never follow the voice of a stranger.[8]
>
> I pray for my brothers and sisters who are reading this book, that You will send Your Spirit to be their Teacher.[9] Lead them in the way everlasting.[10] Teach them—teach me—how to truly press in before You.[11] Cause us to seek Your face![12] Give us a passion for Your presence.
>
> Help us to be still and know that You are God.[13] Give us ears to hear Your still, small voice and to obey,[14] knowing that we can be confident it is Your voice *if* what is impressed upon our hearts is in perfect agreement with Your Word.
>
> Here we raise our Ebenezer and come in confidence of Your empowering help!
>
> In the name of Your only begotten Son, Jesus Christ, Amen!

---

1. Lamentations 3:23.
2. 2 Corinthians 12:9.
3. Matthew 6:33.
4. See 2 Corinthians 1:20.
5. Luke 24:49.
6. Deuteronomy 33:27.
7. John 10:27.
8. John 10:5.

9. John 14:26.
10. Psalm 139:24.
11. Isaiah 48:17; Psalm 73:28; James 4:8.

12. Psalm 27:8.
13. Psalm 46:10.
14. Luke 8:8; 1 Kings 19:12.

PRESSING IN WITH PRAISE

CHAPTER 3

On that first morning, I typed the date at the top of the page and stared at my computer screen. The blank white page glared back at me. This was intimidating. Previous experience in writing expressions of love for my husband had little prepared me to write prayers to God. This seemed dramatically different.

"Father, where do I begin? Teach me how to pray! Teach me how to press in to Your presence!"

Right away I recalled Psalm 100:4, 5: "Enter into His gates with thanksgiving, and into His courts with praise. Be thankful to Him, and bless His name. For the LORD is good; His mercy is everlasting, and His truth endures to all generations."

A royal priesthood

The Old Testament reveals that before God established Aaron and his descendants—along with the entire tribe of Levi—to carry out the duties of the priesthood, God had called *all* of His people to be a kingdom of priests. The setting was the wilderness of Sinai, where the Israelites were encamped before the mountain. God gave Moses these words to take to the people:

> "You have seen what I did to the Egyptians, and how I bore you
> on eagles' wings and brought you to Myself. Now therefore, if you
> will indeed obey My voice and keep My covenant, then you shall be a

special treasure to Me above all people; for all the earth is Mine. And
you shall be to Me *a kingdom of priests* and a holy nation"
(Exodus 19:4–6; emphasis added).

Although the Israelites of old did not follow God's original plan, the same call
is issued for God's New Testament people—under the Lordship of Jesus Christ—
to fulfill the role of "a kingdom of priests":

You are a chosen generation, ***a royal priesthood,*** a holy nation, His own
special people, that you may proclaim the praises of Him who called you out
of darkness into His marvelous light; who once were not a people but are now
the people of God, who had not obtained mercy but now have obtained mercy
(1 Peter 2:9, 10; emphasis added).

Christians are a "royal priesthood"—a fellowship of priests, who are to come
boldly into God's presence[1] through the "new and living way" opened for us by
the blood of Jesus.[2]

Temple priests entered into God's presence in a specific order. First, they had
to enter through a gate to reach the outer court. As I considered this, I pictured
the heavenly temple described by the apostle John.

"Then the temple of God was opened in heaven, and the ark of His covenant
was seen in His temple" *(Revelation 11:19).*

Enter His gates with thanksgiving

God was leading me into His presence through the heavenly portal of thanksgiving. This would be the first portion of my prayer and would be followed by
praise. Since thanksgiving is a form of praise, I later combined these segments
under one label—Praise.

What is thanksgiving? Why should we begin our prayer in this way?

Thanksgiving is a joyful expression of gratitude to God for His goodness toward us, recognizing Him as the Giver of every good and perfect gift.[3] God wants
us to recognize, appreciate, and acknowledge His goodness that we may proclaim
with the voice of thanksgiving all of His wondrous works.[4]

Why? It took me some time to realize how *faith-building* this is. God prescribed the practice of thanksgiving to open our hearts like receptacles—vessels ready to be filled with a greater measure of trust and faith. Let me illustrate this with a story.

The Sunday morning after my 2004 car accident, the problems I confronted set me up as the perfect candidate for complaining. Just twenty-four hours earlier, I had the typical ration of troubles that accompany mortal life, but good health had made it easier to give God thanks.

I had been scheduled that day to preach two services in two different towns, thirty miles apart; one service began at 9:30 A.M. and the other at 11:00 A.M. When I concluded the first service, I departed for the next without delay.

Traveling a four-lane divided highway—driving southbound at the speed limit of seventy miles per hour—I saw a white van pull out from a dirt road. It crossed the northbound lanes and came to a stop in the median. The driver appeared to be looking in my direction, so I didn't slow down. Just as I approached his location, he soared across the first southbound lane and into the second outer lane—directly in front of me!

The van loomed large about twelve feet ahead. There was no time to hit the brakes. That would not prevent a collision anyway. It flashed through my mind that fatalities would result if I broadsided the van. Instinctively, I yanked my steering wheel sharply to the right. Then I saw it. A deep dirt ditch ran parallel to the road, but I was careening directly toward a concrete culvert that had steel rods jutting out from its center.

"Lord, save me!" The only words of prayer that time would permit.

Details from that critical moment forward are a bit blurry. My SUV slammed nose-down into the ditch—seventy miles per hour to zero upon impact! Contents from the back catapulted to the front floorboard. Ricocheting like a bullet, my SUV lurched into the air, made a quarter turn, and bounced violently to a landing. I momentarily lost consciousness. When I opened my eyes, I was surprised to see I was straddling the V-shaped ditch.

I shoved the door repeatedly against the earthen side of the ditch and managed to open it just enough to squeeze my body through. Stumbling upward through weeds, I saw the white van pulled off to the side of the road a couple of hundred yards up the highway. When the driver spotted my head, he hopped into his van and sped off.

Dazed, I desperately tried to wave down two passing cars, but apparently they were not able to see me. I searched for my cell phone, but couldn't find it to call for help.

Observing that the ditch became shallower as it went farther south, it appeared my best option was to try to maneuver my vehicle out of its landing place. Straddling the sloping sides, I cautiously drove a quarter of a mile until the ground graduated in elevation enough to allow for my return to the highway.

Unaware of how seriously I had been injured, I reached the second church as the song service was finishing and preached the message God had given me.

Now, on this morning after, I knew my injuries were significant. Throbbing pain had robbed me of even a wink of sleep all night. My neck seemed hot and swollen—I couldn't turn my head. The slightest movement of my arms caused nerve pain that shot like lightning bolts from the base of my neck to my fingertips. Jammed fingers twice their normal size throbbed, and a torn ligament mimicked a knife being thrust through my shoulder blade. My feet bottoms were bruised, and an egg-sized bump on my forehead explained my headache.

I wouldn't be writing my prayer this day!

I could have murmured against the Lord. *Wasn't I working in Your vineyard when this happened? Didn't I pray for traveling mercies? Why would You allow such an accident to happen?* J.D. was out of town. I was home all alone. Parched and thirsty, I couldn't get out of bed for a glass of water.

Exercising mental gymnastics, I tried to calculate how we would pay for the medical costs sure to come. Benefits through our auto policy would be questionable. There had been no collision, no police report, and no witnesses to step forth. We carried a five thousand dollar per person deductible on our health insurance. Neither policy seemed too promising for payment. This could result in massive medical expenses at a time we could ill afford it. Had I known then it would ultimately cost us eighteen thousand dollars out-of-pocket (our health provider insisted the auto insurer should cover the expenses—the auto insurer saw it differently), perhaps I would have murmured.

But, the point is, I didn't. God had so changed my heart through the practice of thanksgiving that I sensed His blessing in every situation. He had filled my heart with trust and faith, through the experience of acknowledging His goodness.

"Thank You, Father, that I didn't collide with that van and kill someone! Thank You, Father, for saving my life! Thank You for sending angels to carry me beyond that concrete culvert. Had I hit it, I would probably have died. I am so thankful my impact was in the dirt ditch. Thank You for preventing the SUV from rolling over. Thank You that I wasn't injured by the tools or impaled by the fence T-posts sailing from the back of the vehicle. Oh, Lord, I praise You for Your protection! Thank You that I can still walk. Thank You for blessing me with so many other blessings. I give thanks, for I know You will work this out for my good.[5] You have a plan for my life[6]—Hallelujah!"

Monday I awoke to a severe post-concussion syndrome and uncontrollably racing thoughts that seemed true, although they weren't. Eventually, I learned I had cracked the axis of my spine (upon which the head sits) and had two badly bulging disks in my neck. Surgery to repair the damage would leave my head with no range of motion. I opted not to have an operation. For the next forty-two months, constant pain was my companion. Yet, I rarely murmured about my condition. When I was tempted, the Holy Spirit reminded me to continue thanking God for His mighty hand of protection.

Here is our wake-up call. If we murmur and complain against our circumstances, we are actually murmuring against God[7] and forgetting all of His benefits!

King David exclaimed, "Bless the LORD, O my soul, and forget not all His benefits: Who forgives all your iniquities, who heals all your diseases, who redeems your life from destruction, who crowns you with lovingkindness and tender mercies" *(Psalm 103:2–4).*

That Bible passage was my constant prayer! Thanksgiving had made my heart an open receptacle into which God could pour out His blessings. One morning, three and a half years after my accident, there was a stunning reversal of my situation. I woke up and realized the pain was completely gone. I had trusted in God's goodness and He—in His delight of mercy—removed my torment. It has never returned!

Rejoice always, pray without ceasing, *in everything give thanks;*

for this is the will of God in Christ Jesus for you
(1 Thessalonians 5:16–18; emphasis added).

Let us come before His presence with thanksgiving;
Let us shout joyfully to Him with psalms
(Psalm 95:2).

It isn't easy to give thanks "in everything" as Paul admonishes us to do. Not easy, but it is therapeutic. You may have heard the parable of the man who complained he had no shoes, until the day he saw a man who had no feet. In every situation, you have something "more" for which to be thankful than do 90 percent of the world's population.

I'm corresponding with a dear sister in Christ who watched 3ABN on television for years to improve her English. Several years ago, this resulted in her conversion from Islam. I pray for her daily. She is highly educated and lost her job because she refused to break the fourth commandment.

This precious woman lives in a Muslim nation, and her Muslim husband is furious over her conversion. He discovered her Bible buried in the garden and destroyed it, then denied her access to television and removed the computers from their home. He beats her regularly, sometimes sending her to the hospital. Even more horrific, in his rage he has beaten their twelve-year-old son to coerce information from the child about his mother. This mean-spirited man has deprived her and their two children of basic necessities. Yet she continually gives thanks to God for His spiritual blessings.

She is thankful her children are learning to be content with what they have. She is thankful for the character-building life lessons that tutor them. Her seething husband has tried to commit her to an insane asylum. The Lord intervened. Now he has filed a case in the Muslim judicial system to have her sentenced to prison for proselytizing their son, who also accepted Christ as his Savior. If this fails, he threatens to divorce her and take the children away from her—only to place them in an orphanage.

Our precious sister has learned the vital lesson we all must learn. She keeps her heart open before the Lord through thanksgiving. She recognizes, appreciates, and acknowledges God's goodness, and therefore approaches her loving heavenly

Father with a heart filled with expectation. God gives her daily evidences of His love and presence in her life.

This trusting daughter of God believes He will work all things together for her good. She knows and clings to His promises. Like the patriarch Job, her testimony rings out, "Though He slay me, yet will I trust Him" *(Job 13:15)*. Her faith serves as a spiritual telescope that lets her look ahead to a better day. Such full-throttled faith inspires me daily.

Thanksgiving is a faith-builder! It takes our eyes off self and focuses our vision on the Lord. As we contemplate His love for us, it awakens our awe. The act of thanksgiving alters our attitudes and prevents the poor-pitiful-me party.

Are you in emotional turmoil right now? Does this whole concept seem foreign to your mind? I understand, because I have shared your feelings in the past.

Have you lost a loved one? Is it difficult to discover reasons for thankfulness in your grief-gripped heart? Consider thanking God for being capable of grieving—which means you are capable of loving. Consider thanking Him for the time you shared with that special person.

Perhaps you have been victimized, suffering cruelties at the hands of an unsympathetic abuser. From personal experience, I know this can shrivel the heart and stifle thanksgiving. If this is your case, please consider thanking God for His mercies, which are new every morning,[8] and for the better plan He has for your life—which He will reveal as you seek His face.[9]

> He trusts us with a trial in order that He may polish our potential.

Have you been diagnosed with a fatal disease? Does fear squeeze your heart like a vise? Consider thanking God for the blessed hope of eternal life[10] and for the opportunity this advance knowledge provides you to put your affairs in order. Thank Him for the peaceful rest ahead of you as you await resurrection morning—the day you will hear His voice and come forth from the grave to everlasting life.[11] Thanksgiving can quell your fear, adding joy and quality to each remaining moment. Learning to *live* with your condition is better than learning to *die* with it.

Maybe you are facing serious, but more mundane problems. Are you fatigued by financial concerns? Has someone at work molested your reputation with malicious rumors? Then listen to this counsel: "Count it all joy when you fall into various trials" *(James 1:2)*. This is difficult counsel, but learning to heed it has its reward.

Why should we give thanks for fiery trials? The apostle James continues by telling us that trials test our faith and produce patience. When patience is worked out in us, we are perfect and lack nothing.[12]

Crisis reveals character. God sees a greater potential in us. He trusts us with a trial in order that He may polish our potential. God engineers our circumstances for our eternal benefit—working all things together for our good, to conform us to the image of Jesus.[13] As we are tried in the fiery furnace, our faith is purified and fused with patience. Faith eliminates the fog of circumstances. We see God's goodness more clearly, and patience perfects peace in our hearts.

"Giving thanks always for all things to God the Father in the name of our Lord Jesus Christ" *(Ephesians 5:20)*. The luster of our faith-life is marred when we murmur about misfortunes. Did our circumstances escape the attention of the One who knows the end from the beginning?[14] Instead of focusing on problems, focus on the goodness and mercy of the Problem-Solver. He will hear from heaven and will reward your faith in Him.[15] He will keep you in perfect peace![16]

The obvious point here is to develop and maintain a thankful heart. Make a list of your blessings. At the top of your list should be thanksgiving for His indescribable gift—our Lord and Savior Jesus Christ—and the gift of salvation.[17] Thank Him for strengthening you with power through His Holy Spirit living in you.[18] Thank Him for the transforming power of His Word, which—implanted in your heart—is able to save your soul.[19]

"Without faith it is impossible to please Him, for he who comes to God must believe that He is, and that He is a rewarder of those who diligently seek Him" *(Hebrews 11:6)*. When we enter His gates with thanksgiving, remembering His rewards, we will pray more boldly and with increased assurance. Building on the foundation of trust, our faith mounts up on wings! We are ready to approach the Lord in a manner that pleases Him, and we won't risk being guilty of grieving the Lord through ingratitude and disbelief.

Pressing in to His Presence

Consider this for a moment. Have you ever given good things and performed special favors for someone who repeatedly takes your generosity for granted? How do you feel when little to no appreciation is expressed? Be honest! If you have come into contact with an ungrateful wretch like this, the day arrives when you weigh the benefits of withholding your favor to teach the good lesson of gratitude. Isn't that true?

It grieves the heart of the Giver of "every good gift and every perfect gift"[20] when we fail to thank Him for His undeserved goodness toward us. Jesus healed ten lepers. Only one—a Samaritan—returned to offer the thanksgiving due Him. Jesus answered and said, "Were there not ten cleansed? But where are the nine? Were there not any found who returned to give glory to God except this foreigner?" *(Luke 17:17, 18)*.

I wonder if God ever delays answering our prayers because of our lack of thanksgiving, just to teach us the lesson of showing appreciation for all He has done for us through Christ. Thought-provoking, isn't it?

> Therefore by Him let us continually offer the sacrifice of praise
> to God, that is, the fruit of *our* lips, giving thanks to His name
> *(Hebrews 13:15)*.

Enter His courts with praise

> Enter into His gates with thanksgiving, and into His courts with praise
> *(Psalm 100:4)*.

Thanksgiving is our way of passing through the heavenly portal of His temple. We are now ready to enter His courts with praise.

What is the difference between thanksgiving and praise? We have already seen that thanksgiving is a form of praise—a somewhat self-focused platform of praise, as we make a joyful expression of gratitude to God for His goodness toward us. Having thus begun, we are now ready to graduate to a higher form.

The Hebrew word for "praise" is *hālal* and it means to "boast about" and to "celebrate." Nearly every language on earth uses the term *Hallelujah* (also rendered as *Alleluia*), which is derived from the Hebrew *hālal* and is generally translated "Praise the Lord."

Praise is the official worship language of heaven. It is how created beings give God awe-inspired respect for His character traits and all of His magnificent undertakings. It is the first command of the three angels' messages in Revelation, chapter 14.

> Then I saw another angel flying in midair, with an eternal Gospel
> (good news) to tell to the inhabitants of the earth. . . . He cried with
> a mighty voice, Revere God and give Him glory (honor and praise
> in worship), for the hour of His judgment has arrived. Fall down
> before Him; pay Him homage and adoration and worship Him Who
> created heaven and earth, the sea and the springs (fountains) of water
> *(Revelation 14:6, 7, AMP).*

As we consider whom we approach in prayer—the Creator of all—and we offer Him the glory due His name, our expression of praise erodes our own prideful condition. Coming into His courts with praise causes us to recognize our absolute dependence upon Him and teaches us to worship the Lord in the beauty of holiness.

> For the LORD is great and greatly to be praised. . . .
> Honor and majesty are before Him;
> Strength and beauty are in His sanctuary. . . .
>
> Give to the LORD the glory due His name;
> Bring an offering, and come into His courts.
> Oh, worship the LORD in the beauty of holiness!
> *(Psalm 96:4–9).*

"This people I have formed for Myself; they shall declare My praise" *(Isaiah 43:21).* The Bible has much to say about our acts of praise. We were formed, chosen, and commanded to praise God. "You are a chosen generation, a royal priesthood . . . that you may *proclaim the praises* of Him who called you out of darkness into His marvelous light" *(1 Peter 2:9; emphasis added).*

Why does God command us to praise Him? Does He require our praises to feel good about Himself? Do our praises change Him? Certainly not! He has spoken, "I am the LORD, I do not change" *(Malachi 3:6)*. Again it is written, "Jesus Christ is the same yesterday, today, and forever" *(Hebrews 13:8)*.

Praise doesn't change God—praise changes us! It changes our mental prayer posture, making us more respectful as we realize it is our Holy and Righteous Father whom we are addressing. As we offer up our sacrifice of praise, God's authority as Master of our lives and destinies is magnified in our minds. Consider David's words before the assembly as he blessed the Lord:

> "Yours, O LORD, is the greatness,
> The power and the glory,
> The victory and the majesty;
> For all that is in heaven and in earth is Yours;
> Yours is the kingdom, O LORD,
> And You are exalted as head over all.
>
> Both riches and honor come from You,
> And You reign over all.
> In Your hand is power and might;
> In Your hand it is to make great
> And to give strength to all.
>
> "Now therefore, our God,
> We thank You
> And praise Your glorious name"
> *(1 Chronicles 29:11–13)*.

"Be exalted, O LORD, in Your own strength! We will sing and praise Your power" *(Psalm 21:13)*. Praise causes us to recognize the power of God and to remember that nothing is impossible for Him.[21] We should praise God, whether we feel like it or not. Praise changes our frame of reference and increases our faith!

"Why are you cast down, O my soul? And why are you disquieted within me? Hope in God; for I shall yet praise Him, the help of my countenance and my

God" *(Psalm 42:11).* As we recall His wondrous works, praise increases the level of our expectations and heightens the hope in our hearts.

In short, praise takes us from our down-in-the-mouth attitude to one of spiritual joy. As we boast about our loving God, we begin to celebrate in our hearts. God prescribed praise for the benefit of our faith! Hallelujah!

God prescribed praise for the benefit of our faith!

Praise God for His name and His Word, which represent His character and are symbolic of His loving nature and faithfulness.

> O Lord, You are my God.
> I will exalt You,
> I will praise Your name,
> For You have done wonderful things;
> Your counsels of old are faithfulness and truth
> *(Isaiah 25:1).*

> In God (I will praise His word),
> In the Lord (I will praise His word),
> In God I have put my trust;
> I will not be afraid.
> What can man do to me?
> *(Psalm 56:10, 11).*

> I will worship toward Your holy temple,
> And praise Your name
> For Your lovingkindness and Your truth;
> For You have magnified Your word above all Your name
> *(Psalm 138:2).*

There is no limit to the number of things for which we can praise the Lord. As we consider His power and the pure beauty and holiness of His character, praise will naturally well up in our hearts and pour forth from our mouths.

God inhabits the praises of His people

The book of Revelation unveils the scene taking place in heaven right now—all creatures there live in constant praise of the Lord. Enthroned in this atmosphere of praise and worship, our God is still inclined to condescend to those who praise Him here on earth.

"But thou art holy, O thou that inhabitest the praises of Israel" *(Psalm 22:3, KJV)*. The Hebrew word for "inhabits"—*yāshab*—is translated nearly twice as often as *dwells*. When we press in to His presence with praise, God draws nearer to us in a special way. He dwells in our praises! Doesn't the Bible say "Draw near to God, and He will draw near to you" *(James 4:8)*? Consider this incredible testimony from the Old Testament:

> Indeed it came to pass, when the trumpeters and singers were as one,
> to make one sound to be heard in praising and thanking the Lord,
> and when they lifted up their voice with the trumpets and cymbals and
> instruments of music, and praised the Lord, saying:
>
> "For He is good,
> For His mercy endures forever,"
>
> that the house, the house of the Lord, was filled with a cloud,
> so that the priests could not continue ministering because of the cloud;
> for the glory of the Lord filled the house of God
> *(2 Chronicles 5:13, 14)*.

Oh that our times of worship—private and corporate—would be filled with glorious praise and graced with His presence in such a way!

The cloud of God's presence is spoken of often in the Old Testament. This cloud led the Israelites through the wilderness.[22] This cloud descended on the tabernacle to enable Moses to speak with God "face to face."[23] (God covered Himself with the cloud; Moses did not actually see His face—no man can see God's face and live.)[24] Paul speaks of the cloud of God's presence and our need for holy living to remain under its protection.[25]

At the age of nineteen, I actually witnessed the cloud of His presence. Delayed by work, I arrived late to a Friday night Bible study at the South Main Church of Christ. Our pastor had been studying about the Person of the Holy Spirit and His role in our lives, and was introducing the wonderful truths he had learned to those who would open their minds to receive. The topic of God's Spirit had been overlooked in the past by this church.

God had also been teaching the group—a small number of about thirty—the importance of opening the study with worship and praise. Over a period of a few months, our time of praise had continued to lengthen.

Arriving forty minutes late that Friday, I heard reverent singing. Not wanting to disrupt the worship, I stood outside the door until the song had ended. Just as I entered the sanctuary, the pastor began praying. I immediately bowed my head to participate in the prayer of praise to God. After the "Amen," I looked up and saw it.

There—at the right front pews—hovering over this small group was a curious cloud. It rested directly above the people and wasn't present in any other part of the sanctuary. I quietly slipped into the pew behind the others and was awestruck by the palpable presence of God. Years later, as I read 2 Chronicles 5:13, 14, I finally understood the visual phenomenon of that evening.

Do you want God to lead you through the wilderness of this sin-sick world by His presence? Press in with praise!

Learning to praise

Several weeks into my new prayer experience, I was prompted to review the praise sections of my written journals. It was a sad disappointment to read my pitiful attempts at giving God the glory due His name. My praise portions played out like a broken record—heartfelt but repetitious.

Oh, Lord, teach me to give You the glory You deserve! Teach me how to praise You!

I remembered what I had studied about the Last Supper of Jesus. When Christ instituted the Lord's Supper, He and His disciples afterward sang a hymn before they went out to the Mount of Olives.[26] Most Bible scholars believe they sang from one of the psalms recorded in Psalms 115–118, which were traditionally sung at the close of the Passover meal.

Our familiar name for the Bible book Psalms comes from the Greek. It carries the meaning of singing with a stringed-instrument for accompaniment. However, the Hebrew name for the book of Psalms means "praises." This book contains more than half the occurrences in the Old Testament for the word *hālal*—the Hebrew word for praise.

I was impressed to look to the Psalms the next day to learn how to praise. After all, if you think about it, the Psalms could be considered a written prayer journal. David's prayers to God are full of intimacy—an indication of how close he was to God's heart. His passion for God's presence was something I wanted to share.

The next day, I began reading a psalm out loud, then praying it back to the Lord in my own words for my praise segment—creating a personal testimony of what the Lord will do in my life. Going through all the psalms in this manner, I grew in spontaneous praise of the Lord. Praise helped me press in to His presence.

Here is a sample from my prayer journal. I have included the scripture to better illustrate this method. My words are italicized and follow the Scriptures.

PSALM 1

¹ Blessed is the man
Who walks not in the counsel of the ungodly,
Nor stands in the path of sinners,
Nor sits in the seat of the scornful;
² But his delight is in the law of the LORD,
And in His law he meditates day and night.

> *Oh, Father God, I thank You for godly counsel. I thank You for blessing me as I follow Your counsel. I praise You for making Your law of love my delight. Give me an unquenchable desire for Your Word, my Lord. Cause me to meditate on it day and night, for Your Word is inexhaustible. Thank You, Lord, for making it my habit to live in Your Word.*

³ He shall be like a tree
Planted by the rivers of water,

> *Father God, I praise You for planting me. I am rooted and grounded in Your love. By Your grace, I am steadfast. Precious Lord, I praise You and thank You for Your rivers of water. I am spiritually refreshed by Your living water.*

That brings forth its fruit in its season,

I thank You, Righteous Father, that You cause me to bear fruit in Your timing.

O Lord, cause me to remember that by Your Word and Your Spirit, You are doing a work in my heart that You have promised to complete.

Whose leaf also shall not wither;

Most gracious Lord, I thank You that my vitality and courage shall not fade.

And whatever he does shall prosper.

How I praise You for Your plan for my life! In You, and by Your grace, my purpose is ever blooming and growing. Glory to Your holy name!

Please note I didn't use every verse, but only the ones I could easily turn into praise. As I proceeded through the book of Psalms in this manner, I found it necessary at times to read more than one, selecting that which had the most meaning to me. I encourage you to try this. It is a potent process for developing the vocabulary and posture of praise.

As we enter into the divine fellowship of prayer, we are well advised to recall the honor and glory that is due our Redeemer. God invites us to approach His throne boldly,[27] but we should come humbly—realizing the privilege of prayer, recognizing the holiness of the moment, and reverencing the omnipotent Creator who is our adoptive "Abba" Father.

"Let everything that has breath praise the LORD. Praise the LORD!" *(Psalm 150:6).* Enter the courts of His sanctuary—His heavenly temple[28]—joyfully with an offering of thanksgiving and praise.

---

1. Hebrews 4:16.
2. Hebrews 10:19, 20.
3. James 1:17.
4. Psalm 26:7.
5. Romans 8:28.
6. Jeremiah 29:11.
7. Exodus 16:7.
8. Lamentations 3:23.
9. Jeremiah 29:11–14.
10. Titus 1:2.
11. John 5:28, 29.
12. James 1:3, 4.
13. Romans 8:28, 29.

14. Isaiah 46:10.
15. Hebrews 11:6.
16. Isaiah 26:3.
17. 2 Corinthians 9:15; Ephesians 2:8.
18. Ephesians 3:16.
19. James 1:21.
20. James 1:17.
21. Mark 10:27.
22. Exodus 13:21, 22.
23. Exodus 33:9–11.
24. Exodus 33:20.
25. 1 Corinthians 10:1–14.
26. Matthew 26:30.
27. Hebrews 4:16.
28. Revelation 11:19.

PRESSING IN THROUGH REPENTANCE, PART ONE

CHAPTER 4

Completing the praise portion of my prayer, it was time to seek God for the next step to *press in* to His presence.

"Holy Father, what shall I do *now* to come closer before You?"

King David's words flashed through my mind, "Who may ascend into the hill of the LORD? Or who may stand in His holy place? He who has clean hands and a pure heart" *(Psalm 24:3, 4).*

There is no doubt about it—sin erects a barrier of separation between us and a holy God!

Sin hinders prayer! "If I regard iniquity in my heart, the Lord will not hear me" *(Psalm 66:18, AMP).* Take note! The sin doesn't have to be what mortals categorize as major. For example, if a husband doesn't honor his wife as a co-heir of the "grace of life"—dwelling with her with understanding—he is warned his prayers will be hindered.[1]

Worse yet, *unconfessed sin causes spiritual drought.*

When I kept silent . . .
Your hand was heavy upon me;
My vitality was turned into the drought of summer.
I acknowledged my sin to You,
And my iniquity I have not hidden.
I said, "I will confess my transgressions to the LORD,"

And You forgave the iniquity of my sin.
For this cause everyone who is godly shall pray to You
In a time when You may be found
(Psalm 32:3–6).

Of course! I needed to seek forgiveness of my sins. To draw nearer to my holy and righteous Father, I must confess all the ways I had "missed the mark" of His righteousness, and repent. If I did not, sin would spoil my success in seeking God's face.

Five steps of repentance

What is *repentance*? It is more than remorse and a mere confession of sins. How do we truly repent? It is crucial that we understand God's guidelines.

Repentance begins with *recognition* of sin. As we examine ourselves in the light of God's Word, the character of our conduct is exposed. Under the Holy Spirit's convicting power,[2] we begin to think differently—recognizing the foul essence of sin.

As we begin to interpret God's marvelous love and see how we have sinned against Him, *godly sorrow* seizes our hearts. We regret our sins. This godly sorrow produces a change of heart, which leads us to repentance and into salvation.[3]

Confession is our next critical step. This demonstrates we have had a change of mind regarding our sin-sick behavior. Through confession, we seek forgiveness of our sins—acknowledging our need for our Savior.

When confession is accompanied with godly sorrow and a sincere desire to change, God forgives us and cleanses us of all unrighteousness.[4] Hallelujah! Our challenge is to learn to *receive God's forgiveness.* This is how we disarm the devil and extricate ourselves from his quicksand trap of condemnation.

Now we are ready for a 180-degree turnaround, but we can't achieve this by human willpower alone. It is God who gives us the power to *change our conduct*! Repentance is a gift granted by God to the penitent.[5] It is His power working mightily within us that enables us to turn back to Him and do His will.[6]

Let's sum up this five-step process of repentance: (1) We recognize and think differently about ungodly behavior. (2) Godly sorrow causes us to regret our sin. (3) Our attitudes are altered and we confess our sins, asking for forgiveness.

(4) We receive God's forgiveness, applying His healing balm to our wounded souls. (5) God empowers us to change our conduct and make a U-turn in the right direction—straight toward Him!

It wasn't until several months after the Lord taught me the joy of repentance that I recognized God's leading in the continuation of the sanctuary theme in this prayer pattern.

Before the priests of old could enter into His Holy Place—drawing closer to God—they first encountered the altar of burnt offering in the outer court[7] where the sacrifice for sin was offered.[8]

The altar of burnt offering

In this book, I will offer a brief overview—as a matter of observation only—of the similarities between each prayer segment and the ancient sanctuary theme. With that in mind, let's now consider the first article of the outer court and how it relates to our repentance.

The outer court, enclosed by linen hangings, was 150-feet (100 cubits) long and 75-feet (50 cubits) wide.[9] As worshipers entered the court, the most conspicuous item in front of them was the impressive sight of the altar of burnt offering, centered midway between the gate and the door of the tabernacle. Overlaid with bronze, its foursquare form was 7.5 feet (5 cubits) on each side, and 4.5 feet (3 cubits) high. Large "horns" projected from each corner.[10]

The blood-stained exterior witnessed against the guilt and horror of sin, which deserved the wrath of a righteous God. Smoke ascending from a continuously burning fire served as a manifestation of God's mercy and forgiveness, secured through a substitutionary sacrifice. Man did not kindle the flame—the altar had been supernaturally set ablaze when fire came out from before the Lord to consume the very first offering.[11] This divine flame was never allowed to go out[12]—it was transported in a fire pan when the portable sanctuary was moved. This testified to the fact that only God has the power to consume the sacrifice and absolve the sinner.

The altar of burnt offering was also called "the table of the Lord," upon which no imperfect sacrifice could be offered.[13] As part of the daily service, the priests made an offering for the nation that consisted of two male lambs (in their first year and without blemish)—one at the dawn of day and the second at evening.[14] This confirmed the nation's consecration to God and constant dependence upon Him for atonement from sin.

Also on this altar, offerings for individual sins were made. The deaths of the animals demonstrated that sinners deserved to die for their sins, but were reconciled to God by transferring their sins to a sacrificed victim that served as a substitute. A guilty party could also flee to the blood-smeared horns of this altar and cling to them for asylum.[15]

"We have an altar from which those who serve the tabernacle have no right to eat" *(Hebrews 13:10).* The altar of burnt offering pointed to Calvary's blood-stained cross, our New Testament altar—a witness of our guilt and great need to be reconciled to God. The sacrificial animals were a type of Christ, the Lamb of God who takes away the sins of the world[16]—the Lamb slain from the foundation of the world![17]

"The chastisement for our peace was upon Him. . . . The LORD has laid on Him the iniquity of us all" *(Isaiah 53:5, 6).* Christ is both our substitutionary Sacrifice and our Priest. He died the death we deserved that we might live the life He deserves. As our High Priest, He ever lives to make intercession for us.[18]

"Let us have grace, by which we may serve God acceptably with reverence and godly fear. For our God is a consuming fire" *(Hebrews 12:28, 29).* Because we know God as our loving heavenly Father, I think perhaps we take for granted the holiness of His character. Yes, He loves the sinner, but sin is an abomination to Him. Without the blood of Christ covering us, sinners like us could not stand in the presence of a holy God—we would be consumed by His glory.[19]

"You cannot drink the cup of the Lord and the cup of demons; you cannot partake of the Lord's table and of the table of demons" *(1 Corinthians 10:21).* What partnership has righteousness with lawlessness? What fellowship has light with darkness?[20] To enjoy communication in prayer in the presence of our Lord, we must first stop at the Cross—our New Testament altar.

"Knowing that you were not redeemed with corruptible things, like silver or gold, from your aimless conduct received by tradition from your fathers, but with the precious blood of Christ, as of a lamb without blemish and without spot" *(1 Peter 1:18, 19).* Our communion with God is through the blood of Christ. We are accepted in His beloved Son, and in Him we receive the riches of God's grace—redemption through His blood and the forgiveness of sins.[21]

Our daily sacrifice of repentance is the process of applying the blood of Christ, who offered Himself without spot to God, that we might cleanse our consciences to serve the living God.[22] In this way, we grab hold of the Horn of our salvation.[23] We make peace with God through the blood of His cross, and Christ presents us holy and blameless before the Almighty.[24] Hallelujah—this is the joy of repentance!

Anatomy of sin

Before we take a closer look at repentance in chapter 5, let's spend a few moments in the study of sin. Don't sigh. I know this is something you might not eagerly embrace, but I promise it will serve a great purpose and offer a personal benefit to you. The recognition of sin is the beginning of repentance, and repentance brings times of refreshing.

I fully expect the combined teaching of this chapter and the next to make your heart leap for joy! I'll give you fair warning. This will correspond with the joy of childbirth—first comes the *pain* (from solemn recognition of our pitiful sin condition), followed by the *joy* (learning to receive God's forgiveness and recognize His power to change us).

Don't let the devil discourage you as we examine the nature of sin. Don't stop reading until you get through the good part—the God part! He has a solution for our sin problem, and He will deliver us!

I view the word *SIN* as the perfect acronym for what lies at the root of it—(S)elfishness, (I)gnorance, and (N)eglect.

Self-centered behavior causes us to commit sins intentionally—to carry out ungodly conduct even though we know in our hearts it is wrong.

Ignorance is the root of all *un*intentional sins.

Neglect is another intentional act of sin. We know what is right, but fail to do it—perhaps because we are overly busy.

Our great adversary, Satan, has calculated sin to a science. During my schooldays, math and science were my two favorite subjects. I enjoyed the critical thinking those classes required, but had never thought to apply a similar analysis to sin. Sin is the most serious of humanity's problems. Don't you agree we should explore the inner workings of it more carefully so that we may be on guard against it?

Pressing in to His Presence

The Bible spells out the anatomy of sin for us:

> Each one is tempted when he is drawn away by his own
> desires and enticed. Then, when desire has conceived, it gives
> birth to sin; and sin, when it is full-grown, brings forth death.
> Do not be deceived, my beloved brethren
> *(James 1:14–16).*

We frequently apply this passage to so-called pagans, but notice that James was addressing his "beloved brethren." Christians are not immune to Satan's devices. He is masterful at using secular influences to seduce the complacent.

Satan roams around like a roaring lion, seeking whom he may devour.[25] Sin crouches at the door—ready to pounce. Why would we open the door to temptation that we might be trapped in the devil's teeth of tyranny?

In one word—pleasure. Yes, pleasure! Don't be shocked; this is biblical. Unlike the stereotypical picture we paint with broad strokes to illustrate sin as an event bankrupt of enjoyment, the Bible refers to the "passing pleasures of sin."[26] Satan is stalking us, offering us his "sin candy," providing testimonies of sin's pleasure through the media and our peers.

If we don't recognize the nature of sin—how fleeting the pleasure, how devastating the destruction—we will be unprepared to resist the devil's temptation and will yield to Satan's suggestions. (Please consider this as you counsel your children.)

Satan is out to squelch the sacred deposit Christ has placed in our hearts. He schemes to catch us off guard, luring us by deceit and doubt. Beguiled by our own selfish desires, we might blindly choose to follow his downward path of brief pleasure.

Consider King David. God called him "a man after My own heart."[27] Surely it can be said the Lord bore him on eagles' wings and brought David to Himself.[28] Yet David—inflamed by torrid lust—plummeted to the pit of disgrace when he took Bathsheba, another man's wife, to lie with her.[29]

A series of wrong moral choices escorted him further down the path of disobedience and degradation. In an attempt to cover his sin, he plotted to have Bathsheba's husband killed. David was headed straight toward the cliff of spiritual death, blinded to his own condition.

God, in His mercy, sent the prophet Nathan to sound the alarm. Nathan told the king a story of how a wealthy man with many flocks of sheep had taken a poor man's *only* ewe lamb—a cherished possession—and served it up for supper. An enraged David was ready to have the rich man put to death. Imagine the abrupt reversal of his fury when Nathan said, "You are the man!"[30] We will consider this accusation further in a moment.

You and I share a common problem with David. All too often we hastily judge the transgressions of others, while being slow to identify our own sin-tainted condition. Who will save us from our blindness? Who is able to deliver us from the sway of sin?

> Therefore He is also able to save to the uttermost
> those who come to God through Him, since He
> always lives to make intercession for them
> *(Hebrews 7:25).*

Christ is able! He is able to sound the alarm, arrest our attention, and bring us to godly sorrow that produces repentance. He is able to wash away the stain of sin with His cleansing blood[31]—able to save us completely[32] from the sway of sin. If we will abide in His everlasting arms of love, He will rescue us and thrust out our archenemy, proclaiming, "Destroy!"[33]

The sin catalog

I think of myself as a "good" person. Most likely you consider yourself to be basically good, as well. Jesus said there is none good but One—that is, God![34] Perhaps our limited understanding of His viewpoint on sin causes us to think of ourselves more highly than we ought.[35] Many will be refused entrance into the kingdom of God because they failed to recognize their sin and their great need for the Savior.

To better appreciate our need to repent, it is important that we delve a little deeper. Let me share with you a portion of the eye-opening study through which the Lord led me.

Numerous words in the original languages of the Bible are used to define *sin.* Rather than subjecting you to a lesson in Hebrew and Greek, we will review the

English translations of some sin categories.

To sin is to

- Miss the mark of God's righteous requirements (like shooting an arrow from a bow and missing the bull's-eye of the target)
- Transgress or trespass (step over the line)
- Commit iniquity (lawlessness—an intentional or unintentional offense against God's law)
- Commit wickedness (evil)
- Be unrighteous (*any* deviation from God's character)
- Be unclean or impure (includes violent sexual sins)

I don't know about you, but at this point, I was already squirming under the scrutiny of my sin. Although it is not something we like to consider, let's continue for the benefit of knowing how much we need Jesus.

I will comment on eight scriptures listed below that served as a wake-up call to me.

"Whoever commits sin also commits lawlessness, and sin is lawlessness" *(1 John 3:4)*. John relates all sin to the breaking of God's law. The King James Version quotes this verse as "sin is the *transgression* of the law" (emphasis added)—a valid translation. Still, the original Greek is better translated "commits lawlessness," which is an *iniquity*—an intentional or unintentional offense against God's law. *Oh, no! Unintentional offenses too?*

"All unrighteousness is sin" *(1 John 5:17)*. Anything we do that deviates from God's holy and righteous character is counted as sin. Mercy! I knew I missed the mark, but that sounded somewhat mild. This one, however, nailed me in the heart! It strikes me that this Scripture can convict us all.

"So we see that they could not enter in because of unbelief" *(Hebrews 3:19)*. Unbelief is the sin that shut the Israelites out of the Promised Land. How often have we doubted a promise of God? To doubt God's testimony is to regard Him as a liar.[36] No wonder it is impossible to please God without faith![37]

"I say to you that for every idle word men may speak, they will give account of it in the day of judgment. For by your words you will be justified, and by your words you will be condemned" *(Matthew 12:36, 37).* Jesus presents this solemn thought after previously explaining that the words from our mouths reveal the condition of our hearts and characters. Worthless, idle words are barren of the life of God's Word. Truly the tongue has the power of spiritual life or death![38]

"To him who knows to do good and does not do it, to him it is sin" *(James 4:17).* James weighs in on the matter of sin, and his words tip the scale toward sins of omission.

"Whatever is not from faith is sin" *(Romans 14:23).* We are sinning when we are uncertain that God approves of an action, but decide to do it anyway.

"The devising of foolishness is sin" *(Proverbs 24:9).* Perverse silliness is sin. The next time someone shares one of those naughty little jokes, stifle your laughter! If you don't, you are demonstrating approval of the impure and stand equally guilty of sin.[39]

"Wash your heart from wickedness, that you may be saved. How long shall your evil thoughts lodge within you?" *(Jeremiah 4:14).* Thoughts of wickedness and iniquity (breaking God's law) are sin.

Ah, that last scripture is where the rubber meets the road. Even our thought-life can taint us with sin. Actually, according to Christ's reckoning, *the thought is the sin* and the action is the *fruit* of sin. I mentioned earlier something we share in common with David—being judgmental of others while turning a blind eye to our own faults. Perhaps we think we're better than David because we have not committed adultery or murder. Or have we?

Pressing in to His Presence

To Jesus, thoughts of *lust* are the sin—adultery the fruit of sin. To Jesus, thoughts of *hatred* are equal to heart-murder—the act of taking someone's life is merely what grows out of an unclean heart.[40]

There is more to this sin study, but surely our consciences have been pricked enough. Considering God's viewpoint, is it safe to say we are steeped in sin? We may have grown up in church and thought we didn't need much "saving" because we were such good people, but now the blinders are off. We see how much we need Jesus. I pray we will be less judgmental of others, knowing how crushing our own sin-burden is.

It's time to cry out to our heavenly Father for mercy.

> Who is a God like You,
> Pardoning iniquity
> And passing over the transgression of the remnant of His heritage?
>
> He does not retain His anger forever,
> Because He delights in mercy.
> He will again have compassion on us,
> And will subdue our iniquities.
>
> You will cast all our sins
> Into the depths of the sea
> *(Micah 7:18, 19)*.

For someone who once thought she was so good, I have come to appreciate the great number of sins God must cast from me into the depths of the sea. With extreme grace, He wipes out the tremendous and inescapable debt that I owe. It makes me love Him even more!

In Luke 7:36–50, Jesus told a judgmental Pharisee the story of a certain creditor who had two debtors—one owed a little, the other, a lot. Neither could pay what they owed. The creditor freely forgave both debts. Turning to the Pharisee, Jesus asked which of the two men would love the creditor more. The Pharisee rightly assumed the one who was forgiven more.

Jesus related this story in reference to a woman of ill-repute who was washing

His feet with her tears and anointing them with fragrant oil from an alabaster flask. Here is the punch line of Christ's story. The self-righteous Pharisee, who recoiled at the act of the weeping woman, loved Jesus very little. He had not recognized his debt of sin. However, the woman—who had once been filled with unspeakable shame and a sense of unutterable unworthiness—knew what Christ had done in forgiving her great sin-debt. She simply could not contain her overflowing love for the Savior.

Christ concluded, "Therefore I say to you, her sins, which are many, are forgiven, for she loved much. But to whom little is forgiven, the same loves little" *(Luke 7:47).* The closer I press in to the presence of our holy and righteous Father, the more I recognize how sin-tainted I am. A better understanding of His "sin catalog" has brought me to a greater appreciation of my massive debt having been erased by Him. I love Him all the more!

"All have sinned and fall short of the glory of God" *(Romans 3:23).* In the original Greek, the phrase "fall short" represents a continuous action. In other words, we all keep on falling short of the glory (character) of God daily. I know I do. How about you? Doesn't it then seem logical that we should repent of our sins daily?

Rejoice in the *recognition* of your sin-debt! God delights in mercy and stands ready to forgive you. His heart beats with pity for the penitent sinner—He will not leave you with your head hanging low. The greater your debt that He has wiped out, the more you will love Him! Hallelujah!

Confession—the clearinghouse of our conscience

For many years, I have traveled extensively in ministry and interacted with thousands of people following speaking engagements. As you might guess, I can't remember all those encounters. But I vividly recall a young man who chastised me in the year 2000 for commenting on my need of daily repentance.

"You don't understand grace!" he upbraided me firmly. "It's not necessary to confess your sins after you have accepted Christ as your Savior. Jesus has paid the price for it all—past, present, and future!"

Agreeing with the sufficiency of Christ's sacrifice to cover the penalty of all sins, I tried to explain how sin separates even the people of God from Him. God shuts His ears to the unrepentant sinner.[41] He requires that we acknowledge our offenses toward Him.

"I will return again to My place
Till they acknowledge their offense.
Then they will seek My face;
In their affliction they will earnestly seek Me"
(Hosea 5:15).

I shared the story of the apostle Peter at the Last Supper. The impetuous disciple did not want to have his feet washed until Christ explained that if he did not allow it, he would have no part in Him. Peter was suddenly eager for more than a footwashing.

Jesus said to him, "He who is bathed needs only to wash his feet" *(John 13:10).* The spiritual implication of this story is evident. Peter had already received spiritual cleansing. He had not dirtied his entire being by turning away from the Lord and back to the sewage of the world's septic system. Still, in his daily walk, he was not without sin. His soiled spiritual feet needed washing—representing confession of sins and repentance.

The confession of a child differs from that of a criminal. A criminal might confess merely for the reduction of the sentence against him. The child confesses because the wrong he has done brings sorrow and a sense of separation from his loving parent. As children of God, when we acknowledge our sins before Him, we can draw near to our Holy Father without feelings of condemnation.

Once again, this correlates with the sanctuary theme. Before the priests could enter into the Holy Place, they were required to purify themselves, or they dared not enter. They washed their hands and feet at the laver in the outer court,[42] which we will explore in the next chapter.

As vigorously as I defended the need for a continuous attitude of repentance, the young man would not budge from his belief. Somewhere in his past, either he had received an erroneous teaching that cheapened the value of confession, or he had forgotten how to be sorry for his sins.

If we say that we have no sin, we deceive ourselves, and the
truth is not in us. If we confess our sins, He is faithful and just to
forgive us our sins and to cleanse us from all unrighteousness
(1 John 1:8, 9).

The apostle John offers believers the sure word of forgiveness that results from our confession. He uses the present active tense of the verb *confess*. That means John was saying, "If we *keep on* confessing our sins." Confession of sin is stressed in the Old Testament and urged throughout the New.

Never become calloused to the act of confession—it is the clearinghouse of the conscience. It is the prescribed manner for allowing God to purify us, and it results in the renewal of a robust relationship with the Lord.

Are you miserable in your sin? Confession in prayer is the place where misery meets mercy. Bring your sins into His light. You will not be telling Him anything He doesn't already know. As Scripture says, "Take *words* with you" and return to the Lord!

Return to the Lord your God,
For you have stumbled because of your iniquity;
Take words with you,
And return to the Lord.
Say to Him,
"Take away all iniquity;
Receive us graciously. . . ."

"I will heal their backsliding,
I will love them freely,
For My anger has turned away"
(Hosea 14:1–4; emphasis added).

If we walk in the light as He is in the light . . .
the blood of Jesus Christ His Son cleanses us from all sin
(1 John 1:7).

Christ's blood shed at Calvary covers our confessed sins! Hallelujah! This is how God cleanses us from all unrighteousness. His grace changes us from a polluted state to a purified condition, giving us clean hands and a pure heart that we might enjoy the privilege of pressing in to His presence. We no longer wander in the wilderness of sin, avoiding the God who loves us. His mercy wipes away our misery, causing us to believe we are accepted in His beloved Son.[43]

Earlier in this chapter, we considered King David's fall from grace. Now let's look at his reaction to Nathan's accusation, "You are the man!"

A hot-headed, prideful king could have done away with Nathan's head. But, with eyes opened to his lawlessness, David exclaimed to Nathan, "I have sinned against the LORD" *(2 Samuel 12:13).*

David was seized by remorse. He confessed his sin against God and repented. You can read his intense record of confession on this occasion in Psalm 51. This is the model I first used to learn to do the same.

Here is an excerpt from one of my first prayer journals, which contains parts of Psalm 51 paraphrased in my own words:

Have mercy upon me, Father, according to Your loving-kindness. Blot out my sins, according to the multitude of Your tender mercies. Wash me thoroughly and repeatedly in the blood of Jesus—take away my iniquity and cleanse me from sin. I have sinned against You and done evil in Your sight. Please forgive me, Father.

Purge my sins and I shall be clean. Wash me, Lord, and I shall be whiter than snow. Hide your face from my sins, and blot out all my iniquities. Oh, Father, create in me a clean heart and renew a steadfast spirit within me. Do not take Your Holy Spirit from me—do not cast me away from Your presence.

Restore to me the joy of Your salvation, and uphold me by Your precious Holy Spirit. Then help me to teach transgressors Your ways, so that they will also turn to You for life. Deliver me from guilt, Lord, and I will speak forth Your praise. I bring my sacrifice of a broken and contrite heart. You desire only that I should confess my sins and turn back to You. Here I am, Lord! I am ready to return to You. Help me, Father! Thank You for Your forgiveness of my sins.

Like David, when the stumbling blocks of sin have tripped us and sent us skidding down the slippery slope, we should humble ourselves and confess our sins. Although our acts may be directed against others, we should recognize that every sin is against our holy and righteous Father—the Creator of all things.

Constant awareness of our absolute dependence upon God is required. He alone is able to keep our feet from slipping.[44] If we try to walk God's narrow path of life without clinging to His hand, we are incapable of preventing our fall.

David had a heart for the Lord and was sensitive to sin, which make his failures more glaringly alarming. I will borrow one more thing from David's journal to share with you now. This is something to consider as you confess your sins and seek forgiveness.

Clear me from hidden [and unconscious] faults.

Keep back Your servant also from presumptuous sins; let them not have dominion over me! Then shall I be blameless, and I shall be innocent and clear of great transgression.

Let the words of my mouth and the meditation of my heart be acceptable in Your sight, O Lord, my [firm, impenetrable] Rock and my Redeemer *(Psalm 19:12–14, AMP).*

That's what I love about David! His relationship with God was intensely intimate, yet his approach to God was never flippant. He knew as he came before the heavenly throne of God that he must stand in the glorious presence of our heart-searching Lord. David desired a blameless conscience before God and understood that confession is the clearinghouse of the conscience.

Why do so many of us have a careless attitude regarding our confession of sin? We should, when possible, be specific—this demonstrates we recognize our wrongdoing and desire to turn away from it. I don't mean to imply that if we cannot remember all of our past sins and confess them individually that God will not forgive us. That is not true. In these instances, David's prayer, "Cleanse me from hidden and unconscious faults," will serve as our sincere-hearted plea. God will hear and forgive.

God will hear and forgive.

It is shallow nonsense to think we can casually confess and walk away cleansed. If we dare be so presumptuous, we seriously underestimate the cost of sin. The idea of mere confession without regret for our ungodly behavior—without the goal of changing our actions—is not biblical. Let us pause to search our heart and inspect our attitude before we approach God's throne of grace.

Our holy God has a benchmark for behavior—a foundation of laws upon which He bases His government. Any conduct contrary to His laws carries the penalty of death.[45]

So I ask, Does God forgive us simply because He loves us? No! Such forgiveness would make a mockery of His laws and would render Him an unjust judge. If God were to waive the penalty of sin for the sake of love alone, He would violate His own holy standards set in stone and make a mockery of the Cross—our New Testament altar.

God forgives us for one reason only—because His Son Jesus Christ stood in as our Substitute and shed His precious blood at Calvary, paying the penalty for our redemption from sin!

The message of the Bible is clear—God loves all of humankind unconditionally.[46] Still, sin demands the punishment of death. What more could God have done to demonstrate His great love than by sending His Son to die for us—offering the sacrifice for our sins—while we were yet sinners?[47] Forgiveness is offered as a free gift to the repentant sinner, but at a great cost to our Father and our Lord.

I pray we will never again take a dry-eyed look at sin. As you come before a holy God to confess your sins, count the cost of sin! Remember the agony of Calvary. Cling to the Cross! There is no greater miracle, no greater grace, than the gift of divine forgiveness and salvation. You are worth nothing less to God than the unspeakable price He paid for your redemption—the precious blood of His Son!

---

1. 1 Peter 3:7.
2. John 16:8.
3. 2 Corinthians 7:10, 11.
4. 1 John 1:9.
5. Acts 5:31.
6. Philippians 2:13.
7. Exodus 40:6.
8. Leviticus 4:25.
9. Exodus 27:9, 12.

10. Exodus 27:1, 2.
11. Leviticus 9:24.
12. Leviticus 6:13.
13. Numbers 28:31; Malachi 1:7, 8.
14. Numbers 28:3, 4.
15. 1 Kings 1:50; 1 Kings 2:28.
16. John 1:29.
17. Revelation 13:8.
18. Hebrews 7:25.
19. 2 Thessalonians 2:8.
20. 2 Corinthians 6:14.
21. Ephesians 1:6, 7.
22. Hebrews 9:13–15.
23. Psalm 18:2.
24. Colossians 1:20–23.
25. 1 Peter 5:8.
26. Hebrews 11:25.
27. 1 Samuel 13:14; Acts 13:22.
28. Exodus 19:4.
29. 2 Samuel 11:4.
30. 2 Samuel 12:7.
31. Revelation 1:5; 7:14.
32. Hebrews 7:25.
33. Deuteronomy 33:27.
34. Mark 10:18.
35. Romans 12:3.
36. 1 John 5:10.
37. Hebrews 11:6.
38. Proverbs 18:21.
39. Romans 1:32.
40. Matthew 5:21–28.
41. Psalm 66:18.
42. Exodus 40:30, 31.
43. Ephesians 1:6.
44. Psalm 121:3.
45. Romans 6:23.
46. John 3:16.
47. Romans 5:8.

Pressing in Through Repentance, Part Two

CHAPTER 5

In the previous chapter, we began our study of pressing in to His presence through repentance. We considered how repentance resembles the sanctuary service performed at the altar of burnt offering. We examined the anatomy of sin, thumbed through God's catalog of sins, and learned that confession is the clearinghouse of our conscience. The point of that study was to awaken awareness of our need for our Savior and for the Christian's continued attitude of repentance.

> One great reward of confession is confidence—a clear conscience gives us confidence before God!

Let's review the five-step process of repentance: (1) We recognize and think differently about ungodly behavior. (2) Godly sorrow causes us to regret our sin. (3) Our attitudes are altered and we confess our sins, asking for forgiveness. (4) We receive God's forgiveness, applying His healing balm to our wounded souls. (5) God empowers us to change our conduct and make a U-turn in the right direction—straight toward Him!

The first three steps were addressed in the previous chapter. Now we are prepared to advance to the all-important conclusion: the final two steps.

You might wonder why it's necessary to make such an issue of repentance.

Confession is often undervalued by the people of God. We suffer spiritually when we don't understand its worth. One great reward of confession is confidence—a clear conscience gives us confidence before God!

> Beloved, if our heart does not condemn us,
> we have confidence toward God
> *(1 John 3:21).*

I went through a deep season of repentance as I was learning to press in to the Lord's presence. It is a humbling experience to draw near to our holy God—His brightness reveals that the records of our best efforts "to do right" are seriously smudged and stained. Like the priests of the sanctuary service, who dared not approach God without first taking time to be cleansed at the courtyard laver, I learned the vital necessity of confessing sin at the beginning of my prayers.

The shining laver

In the courtyard, midway between the altar and the door of the temple, stood a shining bronze laver—the sacred washbowl of the sanctuary.[1] It was made of two parts. The laver served as a cistern to store the daily quantity of water and released its supply through spouts into its base, which was probably saucer shaped and served as a washbasin.

The finest brass was used to fashion this laver, made from the bronze mirrors brought out of Egypt—donated by the women who served at the door of the tabernacle entrance.[2] The laver's basin performed as a reflection pool, where the priests could see any pollution on their person or garments and could wash it away.

Before they could enter into the tabernacle of God's holy presence, the priests were required to wash their hands and feet in the water from the laver, under penalty of death for failure to do so.[3] They were required to inspect themselves, wash away all impurities, and present themselves spotlessly clean before the Lord!

The application to our daily need of repentance is transparent. We must revere God's holiness and come with purity of heart and clean hands before His throne of grace.[4] Looking into the reflection pool of our conscience, we should inspect our hearts and confess our sins. Without confession and repentance, we cannot have confidence that our worship is acceptable before our God.

"Let us draw near with a true heart in full assurance of faith, having our hearts sprinkled from an evil conscience and our bodies washed with pure water" *(Hebrews 10:22)*. To us, a fountain has been opened to cleanse sin and uncleanness.[5] The *guilt* of sin is washed from us by the blood of the Lamb.[6]

We are washed and sanctified by the Word of God[7] in the name of our Lord Jesus and by the Spirit of God.[8] It is not by works of righteousness that we are saved, but according to God's mercy. Through our daily repentance, the washing of regeneration and renewing of the Holy Spirit will cleanse us from the *pollution* of sin.[9] Let us receive His grace of forgiveness, that we may be spotless before our Lord.[10]

The grace of forgiveness

"We are all like an unclean thing, and all our righteousnesses are like filthy rags" *(Isaiah 64:6)*. It never fails to amaze me when someone asks if I believe in righteousness by faith. Are they kidding? That is the only kind of righteousness there is![11] I'll discuss that in a moment.

The dark motives hidden in the crevices of our hearts can be exposed and brought to our attention only under God's great searchlight of inspection. In His presence, inconsistencies in our conduct are revealed—reflecting cracks in our character.

Actually, I was quite startled at my own sinfulness. As I considered my past, I blushed at the words of my unbridled tongue, at the wanton wastefulness of my resources, at the shame of self-indulgence. I blushed at each time I had flaunted my flesh-nature in the face of a holy God. My face was crimson red as I considered the conduct of my "uncrucified" flesh![12]

On one particular morning, my acts of confession engulfed my emotions and almost overwhelmed me. I think you know what I mean. You may know people who are so focused on their own faults that they become miserable and dejected. They can't see what God is ready, willing, and able to do for them. I came dangerously close to this morbid condition that day, but God came to my rescue by teaching me to receive His forgiveness in faith.

When God impressed me to return to praying His Scripture promises as affirmations of what He would do in my life, He revealed to me that I had missed the point of confession and repentance.

God does not call us to grovel in His presence. Repentance should bring joy!

> If we walk in the light as He is in the light . . . the blood of Jesus Christ
> His Son cleanses us from all sin. If we say that we have no sin, we deceive
> ourselves, and the truth is not in us. If we confess our sins, He is faithful
> and just to forgive us our sins and to cleanse us from all unrighteousness
> *(1 John 1:7–9).*

I marvel at God's mercy, mingled with grace! As we plead to be washed from our wrongdoing, the blood of Jesus Christ cleanses us of confessed sin. God grants us forgiveness—a gift that is precious beyond all price!

> Him [Jesus] God has exalted to His right hand to be Prince and Savior,
> to give repentance to Israel and forgiveness of sins
> *(Acts 5:31).*

He desires that we should open our hearts and *receive* His gift of forgiveness. Grace grants us forgiveness and liberty in access to our heavenly Father—the God of new beginnings. His mercies are new every morning.[13] Hallelujah! Receiving His forgiveness takes our focus from what we have done to what God has done. Our situation changes—no longer must we wander in the wasteland of our sins.

> Forget the former things;
> do not dwell on the past.
> See, I am doing a new thing!
> Now it springs up; do you not perceive it?
> I am making a way in the desert
> and streams in the wasteland
> *(Isaiah 43:18, 19, NIV).*

Calling on God to hear our confession and forgive our sins can be considered a way of rededicating ourselves as His temple. Does it not astonish you to consider that we are the living temple of the living God?[14] Christ in us is our hope of attaining God's glory.[15] He abides in us when we abide in Him.[16]

"Do not cast me away from Your presence, and do not take Your Holy Spirit from me" *(Psalm 51:11)*. David understood that the presence of God dwells within us by His Holy Spirit,[17] unless we have quenched (extinguished) His presence by the continual practice of sin.[18] Even so, once we confess and cleanse our temple, we can ask to be filled afresh by His Spirit.

> So I say to you, Ask and keep on asking and it shall be given you; seek and keep on seeking and you shall find; knock and keep on knocking and the door shall be opened to you. . . .
>
> How much more will your heavenly Father give the Holy Spirit to those who ask and continue to ask Him!
> *(Luke 11:9–13, AMP)*.

When King Solomon—the wisest man who ever lived—dedicated God's temple, he repeatedly called upon God to "hear . . . and forgive."[19] Solomon knew the people would fall short of God's glory, but he trusted that God was ready and able to hear the prayers of the penitent sinner and was willing to bestow the gift of forgiveness to sincere-hearted believers. It was after his prayer of dedication, and the praises of the people in worship, that the cloud of God's glory filled the temple.[20]

For us to be open-hearted and ready to receive the most special gift of forgiveness, we must likewise be convinced of God's ability to hear and forgive.

> If My people who are called by My name will humble themselves, and pray and seek My face, and turn from their wicked ways, then I will hear from heaven, and will forgive their sin and heal their land
> *(2 Chronicles 7:14)*.

Humble yourself! Seek His face! Confess your sins and believe the Righteous Judge of the universe will dismiss the case against you and declare you "pardoned." Then, just as Solomon asked God to clothe the priests with salvation and to arise to His resting place in the temple,[21] you can now trust you have been clothed in the garment of salvation and invite God to fill you again with His Holy Spirit.

" 'Come now, and let us reason together,' says the LORD, 'Though your sins are like scarlet, they shall be as white as snow' " *(Isaiah 1:18)*. God invites us to come before Him, to press in to His presence, to consider our sinfulness, and to repent. Though our garments are tainted with sin, the Creator offers to wash and purify us that His image may be reflected in us with a brilliance superior to the sun's reflection on pure-white snow.

"Wash me thoroughly from my iniquity, and cleanse me from my sin…. Wash me, and I shall be whiter than snow" *(Psalm 51:2, 7)*. David understood God's repentance process and yearned for the blessing of its outcome—God would restore to him the joy of His salvation by cleansing him of sin.[22]

It is "Jesus Christ, the faithful witness . . . who loved us and washed us from our sins in His own blood" *(Revelation 1:5)*. Through repentance, our sin-stained "robes" are washed and made white in the blood of the Lamb.[23] We are redeemed through His blood—receiving forgiveness of sins according to the glorious riches of His grace.[24]

I know the joy of repentance was not fully disclosed in the previous chapter. But, let me ask, Are you getting happy yet? Well, here's something that will make your heart leap for joy.

God forgives and forgets! Let me prove this by Scripture. Here is what God had to say about David, *after* his death:

> You have not been as My servant David, who kept My commandments
> and who followed Me with all his heart, to do only what was right in My eyes
> *(1 Kings 14:8)*.

God was—through the prophet Ahijah—sending a message to King Jeroboam, prophesying the destruction of Jeroboam's house because the king had not followed God with all of his heart as David did. But, wait a minute! David was buried and in his grave. Why would God say that David—guilty of adultery, guilty of murder, guilty of breaking all of God's commandments[25]—had kept His commandments and done "only what was right" in His eyes?

"As far as the east is from the west, so far has He removed our transgressions from us" *(Psalm 103:12)*. God is not a man that He could lie.[26] It seems obvious to me that the only reason God would declare David's absolute innocence is that God forgets the sins we ask Him to forgive. Hallelujah!

Let's look at other scriptures that support this truth.

> I, even I, am He Who blots out and cancels your transgressions,
> for My own sake, and *I will not remember* your sins
> *(Isaiah 43:25, AMP; emphasis added)*.

> "I have blotted out, like a thick cloud, your transgressions,
> And like a cloud, your sins.
> Return to Me, for I have redeemed you"
> *(Isaiah 44:22)*.

> "This is the covenant. . . . I will put My laws in their minds and write them
> on their hearts; and I will be their God, and they shall be My people. . . .
> Their sins and their lawless deeds *I will remember no more*"
> *(Hebrews 8:10–12; emphasis added)*.

As we confess our sins in sincere-hearted repentance, God applies the blood of Jesus Christ to blot out their stain. They are covered and canceled in the memory of God. When He looks upon our record, all He sees is the blood of Jesus. Hallelujah! Indeed, His grace is sufficient![27]

I told you this chapter would bring you joy. Oh, how I hope your heart is soaring right now. If it's not, please go back and meditate on the scriptures in this segment. Ask God to illuminate the truth of the grace of forgiveness in your mind. I can't think of better news to share with you. There are still more wonderful truths we will examine, but—in my opinion—this is as good as it gets!

> I will look to the LORD;
> I will wait for the God of my salvation;
> My God will hear me.
> Do not rejoice over me, my enemy;
> When I fall, I will arise;

When I sit in darkness,
The LORD will be a light to me.
I will bear the indignation of the LORD,
Because I have sinned against Him,
Until He pleads my case
And executes justice for me.
He will bring me forth to the light;
I will see His righteousness
(Micah 7:7–9).

Forgive us, as we forgive others

There is one condition I must add, because Christ added it first. We are expected, even commanded, to forgive others.

Although many would like to sweep this topic under the rug, Jesus was adamant about our developing a forgiving heart toward others. He does not lay down the gauntlet to challenge us to a losing battle. Everything He asks of us, He will empower us to do.

Some Christians are alarmed to learn they must forgive an offending party who has wounded them. Just the thought of it can make hearts race and breathing accelerate.

If this describes you, please be assured that just as God said, "For My own sake . . . I will not remember your sins," it is for your own earthly and eternal benefit that Christ commands you to forgive others. Let's see why.

"Forgive us our debts, as we forgive our debtors" *(Matthew 6:12)*. This is the way Jesus taught His disciples to pray. "And whenever you stand praying, if you have anything against anyone, forgive him, that your Father in heaven may also forgive you your trespasses. But if you do not forgive, neither will your Father in heaven forgive your trespasses" *(Mark 11:25, 26)*.

In Matthew 18:22–35, Jesus told the parable of the unforgiving servant. This man owed a debt of ten thousand talents (about ten millions dollars) to his master. He begged for mercy. The master took pity on him and canceled his debt. Did the servant remember the forgiveness extended him and do likewise?

No, the miserable wretch soon found another fellow who owed him just one hundred denarii (about twenty dollars). Grabbing the destitute man by the throat, he demanded immediate payment, ignored pleas for pity, and hustled him off to jail because the poor soul couldn't meet his obligation. Other servants took note and reported the lack of merciful exchange to his master. The master handed him over to the jailers until his debt could be repaid. The formerly forgiven, but personally unforgiving, servant received a dose of his own medicine.

Jesus concluded His parable with this warning, "So My heavenly Father also will do to you if each of you, from his heart, does not forgive his brother his trespasses."

Does this parable imply, as some people think, that we have to forgive only those who ask to be forgiven? Let me share a story that will shed a little light on this.

J.D. and I once entered into partnership with a globe-trotting businessman from a Middle Eastern country. He was connected with royalty, and his lavish lifestyle made him appear extremely prosperous. Our corporate attorney thoroughly investigated this man's background, and no red flags appeared. We met with international bankers and reputable businessmen who stood as his references, giving glowing reports about the capabilities of "the prince."

We were young and filled with robust naivety. Our dreams were soon dashed—the charlatan we took as our partner was operating an extremely sophisticated international scam.

Following a hunch, I traveled to Europe and spent eight weeks unraveling the web of deceit our so-called partner had woven over the previous twenty years. As it turned out, all who had sung his praises were equally deceived and still hoping to profit from their association with this dubious man and hoping to recoup some of their associated losses.

While sitting in a hotel in Luxembourg, I learned that because I had exposed his dealings, he claimed to have arranged a "hit" contract on my life. The likelihood that the threat was real was confirmed to me by the head of the department of treasury (of a country I will not mention), who was certain the prince had connections to make good on the threat.

During the next several weeks, I did everything within my power to unravel his scheme. I flew from country to country, filled with a great deal of personal anxiety and nervously watching over my shoulder. I couldn't believe it. This was the kind of scenario I associated with fiction thrillers only. Remaining in Europe until my mission was completed, I returned to the U.S. satisfied that I had destroyed his unsuspecting support network, but still frightened for my life.

Our short association with this man had saddled us with $250,000 in debt. We were newlyweds. How long would it be before we again saw the light of day financially? Over the next several months, I gradually began to feel his threat on my life was more bluster than reality. But before my fears subdued, something sinister happened in my heart.

I had never hated anyone in my life—until now. I loathed this deceitful person who had threatened my life and plunged us into deep financial problems. My heart broke for some of his victims that I had met. Government officials, businessmen, and innocents who had been taken in by his charm had their lives capsized in the wake of his crossing. He was, in my mind, the devil personified.

One night, while I was praying for forgiveness of my sins, the Lord said, *"Forgive the prince, and I will forgive you."*

"Lord, You can't really mean that! How can You expect me to forgive him? He hasn't expressed regret or repentance."

"Even as I have forgiven you, you must also forgive him,"[28] God insisted.

"How, Lord? I don't know how to forgive him."

"Pray for his salvation, child."

"I don't want him to be saved, Lord. Let him rot in hell!" (My dear husband wanted me to omit this remark because it was so unlovely and unlike me. They say confession to man is good for the soul, but hard on the reputation. Today, the harshness of my words shocks me. I was at that time—decades ago—an immature Christian in emotional turmoil. The remark stands as evidence of my dissipated state of mind.)

"Pray for his salvation. Forgive him and I will forgive you," God repeated.

"OK, Lord, I will pray for his salvation. But, You know I don't mean it." I wasn't being disrespectful, just honest. God already knew how I felt, so I might as well admit it.

I don't know how long I prayed—a couple of weeks, perhaps—before God worked an amazing transformation in my heart. I saw my enemy as the lost and suffering soul he really was. I no longer regarded him from a worldly point of view,[29] but now saw him from God's viewpoint. Rather than merely mouthing a prayer for his salvation, I pleaded for it and actually meant what I was praying.

God had poured His love and compassion into my heart[30] for this pitiful person. I no longer hated this man. Somewhere in the process of praying for his salvation, I had forgiven him.

Do you think for one moment it made any difference to this calloused con artist that I had forgiven him? He could have cared less. How about me? Did my life change for the better? You know it did. Now I could ask for forgiveness of my sins from God with assurance, and He had restored my peace. I could consider the experience without my blood pressure rising. My heart was again filled with goodwill toward all humankind.

God had instructed me to forgive, not for the benefit of this man, but for my own benefit so that I could become like Him.

Jesus said, "Love your enemies, bless those who curse you, do good to those who hate you, and pray for those who spitefully use you and persecute you" *(Matthew 5:44)*. Why? "That you may be sons of your Father in heaven" *(verse 45)*.

Some of Christ's teachings are difficult for human hearts to grasp. Without the understanding given by the Holy Spirit, we have a tendency to gloss over Christ's requirements. I am convinced beyond measure that God does everything for our eternal benefit, as well as to provide us an abundant life on earth. It would be wise for us to quit questioning and simply obey.

I asked the Lord to give me an illustration that would help me teach the dynamics of forgiving others and how it increases our personal well-being. The example He provided has proven to be a great blessing to me and many others. I hope the following story will help you better understand the benefits of a forgiving heart.

Imagine a mountain stream flowing freely down a lush hillside and across a meadow. The babbling brook is twelve inches deep and about two feet wide. Now, picture yourself stretching a tiny wire across the stream, anchoring it securely on both sides. Someone upstream tosses his brown lunch bag into the water, which floats down and catches on the wire. Soon, another person happens along and dumps more trash upstream, which makes its way to your wire and collects with the other deposits. Several more litterbugs eventually make their contributions of trash.

Over time, the trash tossed into the stream begins to accumulate. What happens to the flowing water? Just like a beaver builds a dam stick by stick, the debris dumped into the stream collects around your wire and dams up the water's movement.

That tiny wire represents unforgiveness in your heart. The litterbugs are people who pass through your life and throw their trashy, hurtful words and actions in your direction. One piece of trash begins to pile on top of another as it accumulates around that tiny securely anchored wire of unforgiveness. Finally, one day you awake to realize bitterness and resentment has dammed your heart, and the living water of the Holy Spirit[31] no longer flows through you. You have become unforgiving—and unforgiven as well.

> "If you forgive men their trespasses, your heavenly Father
> will also forgive you. But if you do not forgive men their
> trespasses, neither will your Father forgive your trespasses"
> *(Matthew 6:14, 15).*

> We have come to know and have believed the love which God has for us.
> God is love, and the one who abides in love abides in God, and God abides
> in him. By this, love is perfected with us, so that we may have confidence
> in the day of judgment; because as He is, so also are we in this world
> *(1 John 4:16, 17, NASB).*

"Father, forgive them, for they do not know what they do" *(Luke 23:34).* How that plea must have echoed through the hearts of those at Calvary. What manner of Man was this?

Love cannot flow through a bitter and resentful unforgiving heart. Christ wanted His heart to remain an open channel of love. God is love. To stand as the perfect expression of God's character,[32] Christ had to maintain perfect love. He forgave those who nailed Him to the cross. Our destiny is to become like Jesus.[33] As He is, so must we be in this world. Our journey begins with a heart filled with His love—a heart that knows how to forgive and be forgiven.

God's gift of repentance

Let's see how far we've come in the process of repentance, combining the lessons of the previous chapter and this one thus far: (1) We have learned how important recognition of sin is. (2) We know godly sorrow is a good thing—it causes us to regret our sin. (3) Our attitudes about sin have been altered, and we have confessed our sins, asking for forgiveness—*remembering also to extend forgiveness to others*. (4) We learned our need to receive God's forgiveness, applying His healing balm to our wounded souls so that we can forgive ourselves.

At the conclusion of these four steps of repentance, the verdict has been rendered—a blood-bought pardon is ours! We stand "acquitted" of guilt—"justified" by the imputed righteousness of Jesus Christ, credited to our account. We are made righteous by faith in what Christ has done on our behalf. Undeserved mercy is ours!

Now we must continue to the final point in the repentance process. Without this step, we would be consigned to hobble along with habits of sin. Our future progress would be hindered. This fifth and final part is where transformation and triumph are forged: (5) God empowers us to change our conduct and make a U-turn in the right direction—straight toward Him!

This step in the repentance process represents *sanctification*—through the *imparted* righteousness of Jesus Christ at work *within* us. As the process of sanctification blossoms in our soul, the seduction of sin withers. With absolute confidence in Christ's ability to save, we develop an unwavering commitment to Him that permits no room for compromise with the world.

The process of repentance is incomplete unless we turn from self to God. Genuine repentance results in the rejection of sin in our lives and the return of our devotion to God. This is not an act we can do by our own power.

Repentance is a gift from God. Receive it with joy!

Godly sorrow produces repentance *leading* to salvation
(2 Corinthians 7:10).

Do you despise the riches of His goodness, forbearance, and longsuffering, not knowing that *the goodness of God leads you to repentance*?
(Romans 2:4; emphasis added).

Him [Jesus] God has exalted to His right hand to be Prince

and Savior, to *give repentance* to Israel and forgiveness of sins
(Acts 5:31; emphasis added).

"Create in me a clean heart, O God, and renew a steadfast spirit within me"
(Psalm 51:10). David was fully aware of his absolute dependence upon God to
give him the gift that would turn him back to God. I praise God for leading me
to Psalm 51 as my model to follow in learning how to press in to His presence
through repentance. He taught me to ask for repentance, just as I ask for forgiveness.

When you ask God to forgive your sins, do you also ask Him to grant you repentance? If not, I hope you will from this day forward! You cannot turn around by
yourself. Repentance is His gift to bestow upon you when you acknowledge your
need of it.

"Even if all are made to stumble because of You, I will never be made to stumble" *(Matthew 26:33).* That was Peter's promise to the Lord. Jesus responded, "Assuredly, I say to you that this night, before the rooster crows, you will deny Me three
times" *(verse 34).*

Oh, how much like Peter I was before I learned to depend upon God for the
gift of turning me around, away from my sin. I prayed and pleaded for forgiveness, concluding with a sincere promise to do better. By sheer willpower I determined to overcome sin, only to hear that old rooster's scratchy voice crowing
over my stumbles by the end of the day. Against my heartfelt determination, I
found I had—like Peter—denied Christ through sin again.

All sin is a denial of Christ! Peter's actions were no worse than ours. In fact,
Peter proved to be more responsive than most Christians are. Just one glimpse
from Jesus' eyes of infinite love disarmed the defiant disciple, resulting in heartfelt
repentance. Peter wept bitterly over his sin.[34] Do we?

Before his boastful promise not to deny the Lord, Peter was a man of bravado.
He paid no attention to the Lord's preceding warning, "Simon, Simon! Indeed,
Satan has asked for you, that he may sift you as wheat. But I have prayed for you,
that your faith should not fail; and when you have returned to Me, strengthen
your brethren" *(Luke 22:31, 32).*

Christ predicted Peter would turn away from Him and have need of repentance. He also assured Peter of His help in returning to Him. What did Peter

learn in the process of repentance? He came to appreciate the need for absolute surrender to God and total dependence upon Him.

The secret to success in our daily walk with Christ is to recognize that apart from Him we can do nothing.[35] Doesn't the Bible warn us that we cannot change ourselves any more than an Ethiopian can change his skin or a leopard its spots?[36] Why do we fail to change after confession of our sin? There's only one reason— we attempt to change by our own power.

"If you live according to the flesh you will die; but if *by the Spirit* you put to death the deeds of the body, you will live. For as many as are led by the Spirit of God, these are sons of God" *(Romans 8:13, 14; emphasis added)*. Please notice that it takes a cooperative effort to put to death our deeds of sin. We must work together with the Holy Spirit to accomplish this. It is His power that makes it possible.

Work out . . . your own salvation with reverence and awe and trembling. . . .
[Not in your own strength] for it is God Who is all the while effectually
at work in you [energizing and creating in you the power and desire],
both to will and to work for His good pleasure
(Philippians 2:12, 13, AMP).

Come to Me, all you who labor and are heavy laden,
and I will give you rest. Take My yoke upon you and learn from Me,
for I am gentle and lowly in heart, and you will find rest for your souls.
For My yoke is easy and My burden is light
(Matthew 11:28–30).

Genuine repentance results in being yoked to Christ and filled afresh with His Spirit. Then, He completes the good work He began in us,[37] as He leads us by His Spirit. Hallelujah! When we surrender control of our lives to Him, God *causes* us to be all that He *calls* us to be!

"A bruised reed He will not break, and smoking flax He will not quench" *(Matthew 12:20)*. Do you feel battered and bruised by your mistakes? Come to Christ—He will heal you. Has your first-love passion for Christ dissipated?[38] Is the wick of your spiritual lamp flickering, smoking, and about to go out? Come to Christ—He will add the oil of joy[39] to your life, and your lamp will burn brightly.

"Repent therefore and be converted, that your sins may be blotted out, so that times of refreshing may come from the presence of the Lord" *(Acts 3:19).* Repentance is a glorious gift from God. It brings times of refreshing that speeds our recovery from the sting of sin and revives us spiritually.

"In returning [to Me] and resting [in Me] you shall be saved; in quietness and [trusting] confidence shall be your strength" *(Isaiah 30:15).* Repentance gives us confidence before the Lord and assures us of His power to save. Repentance brings rest to our weary souls.

There is much more that the Bible has to say about repentance. I will insert some of it in the teachings of the following chapters.

As we press in to His presence through repentance, the sin barrier is shattered, and we are confident that our prayers will not be hindered. God quiets our fears with His love. He invites us to come boldly before His throne of grace to find mercy and grace to help us in our time of need.[40] Our Father, the Mighty One, is in our midst and will save us! He rejoices over us with singing![41]

In chapter 4, we visited the New Testament altar of Calvary's cross and applied the blood of Jesus to our sins. Now, in the spirit of the purification rite practiced by ancient priests, we have symbolically washed our hands and feet at the laver in the outer court.[42] Cleansed, we are prepared to go forward.

We are ready to press further in to His presence and enter the Holy Place.

---

1. Exodus 30:18.
2. Exodus 38:8.
3. Exodus 30:19, 21.
4. Psalm 24:3, 4.
5. Zechariah 13:1.
6. 1 John 1:7.
7. Ephesians 5:26.
8. 1 Corinthians 6:11.
9. Titus 3:5.
10. Hebrews 9:14.
11. 2 Corinthians 5:21; 1 Corinthians 1:30; Romans 5:17; Romans 9:30.
12. Galatians 6:14.
13. Lamentations 3:22, 23.

14. 1 Corinthians 3:16; 2 Corinthians 6:16.
15. Colossians 1:27.
16. John 15:4.
17. John 14:17.
18. 1 Thessalonians 5:19; 2 Corinthians 6:14.
19. 2 Chronicles 6:25, 27, 30, 39.
20. 2 Chronicles 7:2.
21. 2 Chronicles 6:41.
22. Psalm 51:12.
23. Revelation 7:14.
24. Ephesians 1:7.
25. James 2:10, 11.
26. Numbers 23:19.
27. 2 Corinthians 12:9.
28. Colossians 3:13, paraphrased.
29. 2 Corinthians 5:16.
30. Romans 5:5.
31. John 7:38, 39.
32. Hebrews 1:3.
33. Romans 8:29.
34. Matthew 26:75.
35. John 15:5.
36. Jeremiah 13:23.
37. Philippians 1:6.
38. Revelation 2:4.
39. Isaiah 61:3.
40. Hebrews 4:16.
41. Zephaniah 3:17.
42. Exodus 40:30, 31.

Pressing in Through Affirmations

CHAPTER 6

God worked a radical change in my life when He taught me to return His promises to Him during prayer, and to confess Scripture as an affirmation of faith in His ability to perform His Word. This chapter will introduce reasons why affirmations from Scripture are life changing.

Writing this chapter will be a challenge for me. I have written extensively on this topic, and the task of condensing this teaching is daunting. My two previous books are *Exalting His Word* (a teaching on the affirmation process) and *Life Affirmations From Scripture* (the sequel, predominantly a compilation of affirmations).

If you are acquainted with those works, please don't skip this chapter. The previous volumes did not reflect how affirmations relate to pressing in to His presence. Any highlights shared in common will serve as a beneficial review.

If the concept of Scripture affirmations is new to you, I urge you to read at least *Exalting His Word.* My motivation is not book sales, but rather to see you gain a perfect understanding of this practice and reap its transforming power. Through this teaching, God regenerated my spiritual walk. Thousands of readers have testified to the same result. Glory to His holy name!

An intimate relationship with God

" 'My thoughts are not your thoughts, nor are your ways My ways,' says the LORD. 'For as the heavens are higher than the earth, so are My ways higher than your ways, and My thoughts than your thoughts' " *(Isaiah 55:8, 9).*

Pressing in to His Presence

Finite minds like ours fail to grasp the infinite wisdom of God. His thoughts are beyond the natural boundaries of our comprehension. Without the Holy Spirit's help, God's ways are mind-boggling to mortal man.[1] People without the Spirit cry out "Why?" They have not learned to trust God or interpret His perfect love.

"This is eternal life, that they may *know You,* the only true God, and Jesus Christ whom You have sent" *(John 17:3; emphasis added).* What does it mean to "know" God? The verb *know* in this verse means "to understand completely" and conveys the thought of an *intimate* connection or union.

God's great desire is for humankind to know Him as Creator, Righteous Judge, Redeemer, Mediator, perfect "Abba" Father, and gracious Benefactor—to know Him as our Sovereign Lord and the Lover of our souls. God wants us to experience His love, light, life, and power. It is *life eternal* to know Him this way.

> "I am the way, the truth, and the life.
> No one comes to the Father except through Me.
> If you had known Me, you would have known My Father also;
> and from now on you know Him and have seen Him"
> *(John 14:6, 7).*

Jesus tells us that we *can* know God! Through His Written Word, the Bible, God unfolds the revelation of Himself and the plans He has for humankind. Through His Living Word, Christ Jesus, He revealed the exact representation of His character. Jesus is "the perfect imprint and very image of [God's] nature" *(Hebrews 1:3, AMP).*

When we see Jesus, we see the Father! One in thought, purpose, and action,[2] They share an identical personality, character, and motivation.

Christ is empowered to give us eternal life, by bringing us into the knowledge of God. Our entrance to knowing Him is through the Bible. An intimate relationship with the Lord begins with an intimate relationship with His Word.

From 1995 to 2002, the Lord led me into a deeper relationship with Him by revealing His higher thoughts and ways that I might know Him better. First, He introduced intimacy with His Word—providing spiritual food for my growth. Then He called me to *press in* to His presence in prayer—teaching me to exhale the pollution of the world and inhale His sweet breath of life.

"Your way, O God, is in the sanctuary; who is so great a God as our God?" *(Psalm 77:13)*. Next, God guided me through an intensive sanctuary study. There I learned His way of salvation. Finally, He taught me how to walk in the power of surrender to Him, which I will share in chapter 9. Though I had considered myself a Christian for many years prior to 1995, it was through these actions that I came to *know* God and understand His plan.

Perhaps the most curious of all human behaviors is that we can learn life-changing lessons from our Lord, only to abandon their practice later. I'm pretty certain you can identify with this dilemma. It's hard for me to think otherwise—too many audiences I have spoken to have acknowledged this common fault we share.

God teaches us a better way, and we walk joyfully in its path for a while, only to awaken one day and realize we are no longer following His lesson plan. To my point, God revealed to me the transforming power of His Word when He taught me to make affirmations from His Scriptures. It was a life-changing experience. For two years, I walked so closely with Him I could sense His heartbeat.

Of course, you know what happened afterward—I shared the saga of my misplaced priorities in chapter 1. Slaving nonstop for a start-up company, I abandoned the affirmation practice for eighteen months and found myself distanced from God. He graciously corrected my backsliding in September 1999, when He called me to pray an hour each morning—teaching me to press in to His presence.

During the first fourteen mornings of this special prayer time, I learned to praise, experienced deep repentance, and assumed the role of an earnest intercessor. God even opened my spiritual ears to identify His still, small voice. Yet, I continued to lack sufficient spiritual power to walk victoriously throughout the day with Christ.

On the fifteenth morning, my problem became evident. I had unplugged from my spiritual power source—affirmations from Scripture! When I added a generous portion of affirmations to my daily prayer, the dynamics of my Christian walk were immediately changed. In a flash, I was infused with faith and went from pitiful to powerful. Once again, I was a Word warrior—armed with the sword of the Spirit and ready to defend myself against the enemy!

Bread of life in the Holy Place

Several months later (January 2000), the Lord led me through the sanctuary study. This opened my eyes to the sanctuary theme in the PRAISE prayer-pattern. Let's review how it has related thus far.

As we began our journey to press in before His throne of grace, we started with the praise segment. We entered His gates with thanksgiving in our hearts and His courts with the praise due our holy God.

Our next steps correlated to actions conducted in the outer court of the sanctuary. We embraced repentance—confessing our sins and pleading the blood of Jesus over our failures, equating this to the symbolism the altar of burnt offering represented. Like the priests of old purifying themselves at the laver, we washed our spiritual hands and feet in the act of repentance, permitting us to draw nearer to our holy God.

Had we been a Levite priest, we would now be ready to enter into the tent of the ancient sanctuary, which was much more beautiful on the interior than the exterior—just as God's people are. It is generally agreed that the sanctuary was forty-five feet long (thirty cubits) and fifteen feet wide (ten cubits), two-thirds of this space was dedicated to the Holy Place, the first compartment, which measured thirty by fifteen feet. The Holy Place contained three items: the table of showbread,[3] the golden altar of incense,[4] and the golden candlestick.[5]

I compare the act of making affirmations from Scripture to symbolic entry into the Holy Place and the setting out of the showbread. Let me first explain this service in the earthly sanctuary.

Twelve loaves (one for each tribe of Israel) were prepared fresh on the Sabbath of each week[6] and arranged in two stacks (of six each) on the table in the Holy Place. An act of worship, this labor was not considered Sabbath breaking. The loaves were flatbread, baked without leaven.[7] (Leaven was a type of fermentation, like yeast, that caused bread to rise. During Bible times, it was viewed as a symbol of corruption or evil influence.) On top of each stack was placed a golden cup of frankincense, which was burned on fire coals as an offering to the Lord when the showbread was changed.[8]

The loaves were a thank offering and a memorial of God's constant provision for nourishment. Because they were set out before the Lord, the loaves were called showbread (*shewbread*, KJV), and were also referred to as the "bread of His presence" or "holy bread." As new showbread was set out each Sabbath, the previous loaves were removed and eaten by the priests in the Holy Place. "They shall eat it in the holy place: for it is most holy unto him" *(Leviticus 24:9, KJV)*.

Let's consider why I compare affirmations from Scripture to the showbread.

1. Jesus is the Word of God incarnate and the "bread of life"!

> **John 1:14**—The Word became flesh and dwelt among us, and we beheld His glory, the glory as of the only begotten of the Father, full of grace and truth.

> **John 6:35**—Jesus said to them, "I am the bread of life. He who comes to Me shall never hunger."

2. God's Word is our *spiritual* bread, given to us as a constant provision for nourishment to maintain vibrant spiritual lives. As we partake of His "holy bread" (His promises), we ingest the "bread of His presence" and partake of His divine nature.

> **Matthew 4:4**—But He answered and said, "It is written, '*Man shall not live by bread alone, but by every word that proceeds from the mouth of God*' " (emphasis added).

> **Jeremiah 15:16**—Your words were found, and I ate them, and Your word was to me the joy and rejoicing of my heart; for I am called by Your name, O Lord God of hosts.

> **2 Peter 1:4**—By which have been given to us exceedingly great and precious promises, that through these you may be partakers of the divine nature.

Affirmations are simply taking Bible promises (*symbolic* "holy bread," without leaven) and setting them out before God in a *symbolic* "table of showbread" offering.

Pressing in to His Presence

This serves as our memorial of His constant provision of spiritual nourishment for us.

Affirmations are more than mere prayer requests. We return God's Word to Him as a thank offering—a declaration of faith that we agree with God's testimony and acknowledge His Word as truth. We confess who we are "in Christ," resulting in personal application of God's promises.

Reaching this point of pressing into His presence, our confession of God's Word can be likened to the priests eating the showbread in the Holy Place. Like Jeremiah, as we "eat" God's Word in this manner, it becomes the joy and rejoicing of our hearts.

"I have not departed from the commandment of His lips; I have treasured the words of His mouth more than my necessary food" *(Job 23:12)*. Even God's commandments are promises of what He will perform in our lives. It is God who is working in us to will and to act according to His good pleasure.[9] He will *cause* us to be all that He has *called* us to be.

There is transforming power in the Word of God! In fact, God guarantees as you partake of His promises, you will partake of His divine nature. His Word will become your testimony and the treasure of your heart.

God sustains us by His Word

In 1995, when God first instructed me to make affirmations from His promises in regard to a health issue I suffered, I recited them with reverent devotion night after night—returning His Word to Him in the form of prayer. Soon, I struggled with self-doubt. Had the Lord really directed me to do this? Faith seemed to be just beyond my grasp.

"Oh, Father," I cried, "help my unbelief." The Lord led me to three verses that created a fireworks display of faith in my heart.

> So shall My word be that goes forth from My mouth;
> It shall not return to Me void,
> But it shall accomplish what I please,
> And it shall prosper in the thing for which I sent it
> *(Isaiah 55:11)*.

Then said the Lord to me, You have seen well,
for I am alert and active, watching over My word to perform it
(Jeremiah 1:12, AMP).

God, who gives life to the dead and calls those things
which do not exist as though they did
(Romans 4:17).

These verses leaped from their pages and into my heart! I understood God's plan for practicing affirmations from Scripture. He was directing me to return His Word to Him, and His Word was not without power, but would accomplish His purposes in my life. Why? He was watching over His Word to perform it. Watching and waiting for me to believe His testimony.

Although my testimony of "Word" confession differed from what I then experienced in the physical realm, I understood that faith begins where sight ends. God's words are spoken with the power of His promise to fulfill them. They are a pledge to His people. I was learning to speak like my heavenly Father—calling things that did not exist as if they already did exist. Isn't that the essence of faith?

Now faith is the assurance (the confirmation, the title deed) of the things
[we] hope for, being the proof of things [we] do not see and the conviction
of their reality [faith perceiving as real fact what is not revealed to the senses]
(Hebrews 11:1, AMP).

God's Word is endowed with life-giving, creative power. Just think about it. How did God create the world? He spoke it into existence—creating something from nothing. Everything "God said" happened *(see Genesis, chapter 1)!*

His Word has the same creative power today as it did "in the beginning," and it was doing a work within me. Although I had yet to see the evidence, faith was being formed in my heart.

"For the word of God is living and powerful, and sharper than any two-edged sword, piercing even to the division of soul and spirit, and of joints and marrow, and is a discerner of the thoughts and intents of the heart" *(Hebrews 4:12).* A study of the Greek text revealed something remarkable about this familiar verse.

In the Greek, the term for "two-edged" is *distomon*. Its literal translation is "two-mouthed" (like a double-mouthed river). Please carefully consider the following affirmation from Scripture that the Lord inspired me to write.

He has given me the authority and eternal power of His Word.
His Word is alive, active, immovable, unshakable.
His Word is a two-edged sword—
the first edge struck when He spoke it;
the second edge strikes when I speak it.
As I speak the Word, I hear the voice of the Lord.
I am returning His Word to Him, and His Word does not return void,
but accomplishes every purpose for which He sent it.
He actively watches over His Word to make certain it is fulfilled
at the perfect time which He has appointed.
(Derived from Hebrews 4:12; Isaiah 55:9–11, 13; Jeremiah 1:12; Luke 1:20;
Habakkuk 2:3.)

What is the primary way God speaks to us? Through His Word! As we include affirmations from Scripture in our time of prayer, we are entering into a two-way communication with our Lord. The Word of God becomes "two-mouthed" as we make it the confession over our lives. Scripture affirmations become alive and active within us.

- Affirmation goes **beyond claiming.**
- It is a **confession**—a word of faith—that **declares we agree** with God's wisdom.
- Confessing His Word **confirms** that it is our life source.
- It **causes** His way of thinking to become our way of thinking.

God's Word has more than *creative* power—it has *sustaining* power. We have already considered how Christ is the exact representation of the Father. Let's look at the second half of that scripture now.

He is the perfect imprint and very image of [God's] nature,
upholding and maintaining and guiding and propelling
the universe by His *mighty word of power*
(Hebrews 1:3, AMP; emphasis added).

Christ sustains us by His Word power! We plug in to our power source when we speak affirmations from Scripture.

You will recall the precious sister I mentioned in chapter 3—the Muslim woman, converted to Christianity after watching 3ABN to improve her English. The reason she can praise the Lord under severe persecution is that she developed full-throttled faith by plugging in to her power source.

On my desk, as a constant reminder, sits a small four-by-three-inch notebook that once was her treasured possession. She "smuggled" it out of her Muslim nation to me. The story she shared in her enclosed letter caused tears to flow down my cheeks.

A small Adventist church in her area serves a group of international Christians who work in her country. When our sister's husband burned her Bible, denied access to the television, and disconnected Internet service to their home, the church members stepped forward. Although they had only a brief association with her, they loved her enough to send Bible verses daily through text messaging.

Her notebook contains those Bible promises she cherished with a passion—written in her own hand, mostly in English. Day and night, she kept this little Bible journal next to her body, hidden under her clothes. It was the only safe hiding place. Her husband ransacks their home regularly to make certain she has no Christian materials. However, he does not touch her—except to beat her.

An event happened that determined it was no longer safe to keep this notebook. Her recordings of Scripture were so precious to her that she could not bear to throw it away. Because she had learned to make affirmations from Scripture by watching a program I host on 3ABN, *Exalting His Word* (titled as my book), she wanted me to have it. Can you imagine how precious this tiny notebook is to me?

Ephesians 6 instructs us to put on the armor of God. In verse 17, we are told that the sword of the Spirit is the Word of God. This sister reminds me of Eleazar, a highly esteemed mighty man of King David. The Bible says, "He arose and attacked the Philistines until his hand was weary, and his hand stuck to the sword. The LORD brought about a great victory that day" *(2 Samuel 23:10)*.

Let us likewise cling to the sword—the sword of the Spirit, the Word of God. When our flesh is too weak, God will become our strength and keep our hand "stuck to the sword." If we'll apply the double-edged ("two-mouthed") principle to our lives, He will bring us victory, cutting us free from the cords of the wicked that try to bind us.

When the tempter tries to trip you and entangle your feet in his snare, pull out your sword and say,

> **It is written**—I am dead to sin, but alive to God. I am under the power of His grace, and sin shall not be my master. I have put on Christ, and I will make no provision for my flesh. God has given me the victory through my Lord Jesus Christ *(Romans 6:11, 14; 13:14; 1 Corinthians 15:57, paraphrased)*.

When the enemy tries to cloud your mind with confusion, pull out the sword of the Spirit and say,

> **It is written**—God is not the author of confusion, but of peace. I have not been given a spirit of fear. God has given me a spirit of power and of love and of sound mind. God is righteous—He has cut me free from the cord of the wicked *(1 Corinthians 14:33; 2 Timothy 1:7; Psalm 129:4, paraphrased)*.

Christ will sustain you with His mighty Word of power, as you learn to wield the sword of the Spirit.

Sustaining power is marvelous, but equally as wonderful is that Jesus uses the Word to wash the influences of the world from your mind.

> Christ also loved the church and gave Himself for her,
> that He might sanctify and cleanse her with the *washing
> of water by the word*, that He might present her to Himself

a glorious church, not having spot or wrinkle or any such
thing, but that she should be holy and without blemish
(Ephesians 5:25–27; emphasis added).

"If you abide in Me, and My words abide in you, you will ask what you desire, and it shall be done for you" *(John 15:7)*. Abiding in the Word of God is a way to abide in Christ. As His promises enter your heart, your mind is transformed. God's thoughts become your thoughts. His desires become your desires. You want to do all things for His glory. Prayers are no longer vain babbling. You ask for His action according to His revealed will in Scripture.

Now this is the confidence that we have in Him,
that if we ask anything *according to His will,* He hears us.
And if we know that He hears us, whatever we ask,
we know that we have the petitions that we have asked of Him
(1 John 5:14, 15; emphasis added).

Praying His Word back to Him is the sure way of praying according to His will. He promises to *watch* over it to *perform* it—it will accomplish the purposes for which He sent it. Praying the Word brings powerful results!

The transforming power of affirmations

This segment will be rich with Scripture. Take your time to slowly chew this "bread of His presence."

Socrates said, "Knowing thyself is the height of wisdom." That sounds smart on the surface, but I beg to differ with this famous philosopher. Jesus said that to know God (and Jesus Christ, whom He sent) is eternal life. Knowledge of God is superior in wisdom to knowledge of self.

That being said, I will add—in the vein of Socrates' thought—it is vitally important for Christians to understand who we have become, now that we are "born again . . . through the word of God which lives and abides forever" *(1 Peter 1:23)*. We have a new "born-again identity" in Christ!

A serious situation exists in today's church. I call it an "identity crisis." This is not mere psychobabble terminology. Our crisis of identity is a critical problem that causes Christians to suffer spiritual defeat.

What is our identity crisis? We don't know who or what we have been re-created to be in Christ! Like ten of the twelve men who spied out the Promised Land, we suffer from the "grasshopper identity syndrome," thinking the giants in the land are greater than we who walk with God.[10] We don't consider the Lord's promise and power to change our nature.

"Therefore, if anyone is in Christ, he is a new creation; old things have passed away; behold, all things have become new" *(2 Corinthians 5:17)*. God's testimony of what He has done for us in Christ is sure. Our destiny is to become like Him,[11] and it's not a matter of chance, but choice!

We must choose each day to accept by faith what God has said. Without faith we cannot please Him.[12] Little wonder. If we doubt His testimony, we are regarding Him as a liar![13]

Our problem is that we don't always feel like a new creation. Harassed by the devil, our old flesh nature sometimes rears its ugly head. Suddenly, feelings overcome faith, making it difficult to believe the old has passed away and the new has come. We begin to think and speak about ourselves in a way that doesn't line up in agreement with God's Word.

"For as he thinks in his heart, so is he" *(Proverbs 23:7)*. What you think of yourself is important. Do you see yourself as a spiritual failure? Continue with this frame of mind and you will never be anything but. God does not force His will upon you—He asks you to choose.

To become Christlike, you must recognize your new identity in Him and seize hold of your destiny. How? By faith accept what God promises, surrendering your lower thoughts to His higher thoughts.

For as many as are the promises of God, they all find
their Yes [answer] in Him [Christ]. For this reason
we also utter the Amen (so be it) to God through Him
(2 Corinthians 1:20, AMP).

By the grace of God I am what I am,
and His grace toward me was not in vain
(1 Corinthians 15:10).

The apostle Paul gives us the answer. We become like Christ by the grace of God. His grace is more than spiritual favor—it is supernatural assistance and the power of God unto salvation! By the transforming power of His Spirit and His Word we change. Every promise God has made He will also perform in our lives, if we accept them by faith.

"Death and life are in the power of the tongue" *(Proverbs 18:21)*. What you speak into your life is important. Speak life by speaking God's Word, and He will reprogram your thoughts. You will possess a spirit of faith and will speak in the spirit of faith. "And since we have the same spirit of faith, according to what is written, '*I believed and therefore I spoke,*' we also believe and therefore speak" *(2 Corinthians 4:13; emphasis added)*.

Affirmations from Scripture will charge your spiritual battery and fill your heart with hope. The word *hope* in the original Bible language did not refer to mere wishful thinking—it meant "eager expectation." Do winds of strife ever come sweeping across your life, stirring waves of overwhelming circumstances? Hope in God will be the anchor for your soul,[14] keeping you steadfast. You will draw near to God without being double-minded (which is a condition to avoid if you expect to receive anything from the Lord).[15]

> *"The word is near you, in your mouth and in your heart"*
> (that is, the *word of faith* which we preach). . . .
> For with the heart one believes unto righteousness,
> and with the mouth confession is made unto salvation
> *(Romans 10:8–10; emphasis added)*.

Affirmations plant God's "word of faith" in your heart and mouth to prevent double-minded confession.

"So then faith comes by hearing, and hearing by the word of God" *(Romans 10:17)*. God's promises are waiting in the wings for fulfillment. They are ushered in by faith. As you take His Scriptures, setting them out before Him in prayer as showbread and confessing them over your life, affirmations will add fuel to your faith. His Word becomes your testimony of your new identity.

Hearing your own voice speak His powerful truths is a great faith-builder. It is a way to "plug in" to the power source of His life-giving Word. Affirmations are the most efficient connection. When you plug in, they transfer His mighty energy, and you are converted to His way of thinking.

I could tell you all day long that you are a new creation in Christ, but you might think, *Shelley doesn't really know me.* However, things are stirred in the spiritual realm when you make an affirmation from God's Word and, speaking aloud say the following:

> I am a new creation in Christ—the old has gone and the new has come.[16] God is working in me to cause me to will and to act according to His good pleasure.[17] He will complete the good work He has begun in me.[18]

It's not easy to accept at first—your mind resists what God says about you. But God declares the end from the beginning,[19] because He knows what He will work in you. As you accept God's higher knowledge, He multiplies grace and peace to you. His divine *power* works in your heart—you become a partaker of His divine *nature.*

> Grace and peace be multiplied to you in the knowledge of God
> and of Jesus our Lord, as His divine power has given to us all things
> that pertain to life and godliness, through the knowledge of Him
> who called us by glory and virtue, by which have been given to us
> exceedingly great and precious *promises, that through these*
> *you may be partakers of the divine nature,* having escaped the
> corruption that is in the world through lust
> *(2 Peter 1:2–4; emphasis added).*

Jesus said, "Did I not say to you that if you would believe you would see the glory of God?" *(John 11:40). As you partake of His promises, you partake of the life-giving, transforming power of His Word.* Your thoughts begin to line up with His thoughts and your will, with His will. Praying and confessing God's promises as affirmations plants His Word in your heart like nothing else can. It takes root, sprouts, and eventually blossoms into reality.

And He said, "The kingdom of God is as if a man should scatter seed on the ground, and should sleep by night and rise by day, and the seed should sprout and grow, he himself does not know how. For the earth yields crops by itself: first the blade, then the head, after that the full grain in the head"
(Mark 4:26–28).

"The seed is the word of God"
(Luke 8:11).

The potential of any harvest is wrapped inside the seed. Plant corn—reap corn. Plant wheat—reap wheat. This is likewise true in the spiritual realm. All of your potential is wrapped inside His seed! Plant God's Word—reap His divine nature. The "seed" of Scripture has miracle-working power to renew our minds.

"Therefore lay aside all filthiness and overflow of wickedness, and receive with meekness the implanted word, which is able to save your souls" *(James 1:21).* Affirmations are the most productive way I have ever practiced the planting of God's Word.

Another kingdom principle is that you become what you behold. Look into the Bible and see who God says you are, now that you have been born again. Our mirror is the Word of God—it reflects the vision of our new nature. Our mirror image is Christ Jesus. As you continue to behold, God will lead you from one level of His glory (His character) to the next, by the power of His Word and His Spirit.

And all of us, as with unveiled face, [because we] *continued to behold [in the Word of God]* as in a mirror the glory of the Lord, are constantly being transfigured into His very own image in ever increasing splendor and from one degree of glory to another; [for this comes] from the Lord [Who is] the Spirit
(2 Corinthians 3:18, AMP; emphasis added).

"Let this mind be in you which was also in Christ Jesus" *(Philippians 2:5).* That is a tall order from the apostle Paul. Who can fill it? Only God can, and He already has. Paul tells us elsewhere that we have been given the mind of Christ.[20]

Pressing in to His Presence

Oh, I want it! I need it. Don't you? How do we receive it? The mind of the *Living* Word, our Lord Jesus Christ, is represented in His *Written* Word.

The seed of the miracle is in the Word of God. As you partake of His promises, you partake of His divine nature. The more you confess the Word of God, the more you begin to think with the mind of Christ. Think like Him, and you will act like Him.

> Do not be deceived, God is not mocked; for whatever a man sows,
> that he will also reap. For he who sows to his flesh will of the flesh
> reap corruption, but he who sows to the Spirit will of the Spirit reap
> everlasting life. And let us not grow weary while doing good,
> for in due season we shall reap if we do not lose heart
> *(Galatians 6:7–9).*

> It is the Spirit who gives life; the flesh profits nothing.
> The words that I speak to you are spirit, and they are life
> *(John 6:63).*

Do you want to reap everlasting life? Sow the seed of God's Word into your heart. Do you want His life-source to be active in you? Open your spiritual mouth and eat His Word; then confess it with your living voice. In this manner, affirmations can be compared to the priests of old eating the "bread of His presence" (the showbread) in the Holy Place.

"Trust in the LORD with all your heart, and lean not on your own understanding; in all your ways acknowledge Him, and He shall direct your paths" *(Proverbs 3:5, 6).* If we're not going to lean on our understanding, then whose understanding shall be our foundation? God's alone—as found in the Bible!

From our limited human understanding, much of what God says seems impossible of fulfillment. His thoughts are higher than ours. We must strive to know Him by accepting His Word with total trust—believing in the Bible as testimony from Almighty God, who cannot lie.

Let's summarize a few points we have learned.

• Affirmation goes beyond claiming.

- Affirmations are calling things that are not, as though they already existed.
- Affirmation is a confession—a word of faith—that declares we agree with God's wisdom.
- Confessing His Word confirms that it is our life-source.
- Confessing His Word causes His way of thinking to become our way of thinking.
- Planting and practicing His promises validate God's testimony.
- As we return God's Word to Him, it will accomplish His purposes.
- God watches over His Word to perform it.

This practice during our time of pressing in to His presence is like setting out the loaves on the "table of showbread." Affirmations serve as a memorial that God is the Provider of our spiritual nutrition. We are reminded of His faithfulness. As we speak with the spirit of faith, God is pleased.

Now I will set the table for us and close with a prayer of affirmations from Scripture (I have included Scripture notations for your ease of reference). I invite you to pray this prayer with me and encourage you to pray aloud, if possible.

O God, You are my God. Earnestly I seek You. Teach me to press in to Your presence. My soul thirsts for You. Because Your love is better than life, my lips glorify You *(Psalm 63:1–4)*. Father, You love me with an everlasting love. Draw me by Your love, and cause me to receive this indescribable gift *(Jeremiah 31:3)*.

I am seeking You with all of my heart, because I know You have a plan for my life that is better than the one I'm living. Thank You, Lord, that I'm assured I will find You *(Jeremiah 29:11–14)*.

You are my God, who teaches me what is best for me, who directs me in the way I should go *(Isaiah 48:17)*. You will show me the path of life, and I know I will find fullness of joy in Your presence *(Psalm 16:11)*.

You have set before me life-and-death choices—I choose life, Father. I choose to love You and obey Your voice. I will cling to You, because You are my life *(Deuteronomy 30:19, 20)*. I trust You with all of my heart,

Lord, and will lean on Your Word for understanding. Help me to acknowledge You in every area of my life. Thank You for directing my paths *(Proverbs 3:5, 6)*.

Father, I am so grateful that You have equipped me to do Your will and that You are working in me to make me pleasing in Your sight, through Christ Jesus *(Hebrews 13:20, 21)*. I praise Your faithfulness. You have promised to sanctify me completely and preserve me blameless at the coming of our Lord Jesus Christ—and You will do it. Hallelujah! *(1 Thessalonians 5:23–25)*.

I have received abundance of grace and of the gift of righteousness. Because of You, I will reign in life through Christ Jesus! *(Romans 5:17)*.

I will not fear, for You have redeemed me. You have called me by my name, and I belong to You. When I pass through troublous waters, You will be with me—they shall not overflow me. When I walk through fiery trials, I will not be burned, nor will the flame scorch me. You are my God, the Holy One. I am precious in Your sight, and You love me *(Isaiah 43:1–4)*.

Thank You for supplying "Word seed" for sowing and the "bread of life" for spiritual nourishment. I pray You will multiply Your seed to me and increase the fruits of my righteousness *(2 Corinthians 9:10)*.

In Jesus' holy name, Amen and Amen!

---

1. 1 Corinthians 2:14.
2. John 10:30.
3. Exodus 25:23–29.
4. Exodus 30:1–11.
5. Exodus 25:31–39.
6. Leviticus 24:5–9; 1 Chronicles 9:31, 32.
7. Leviticus 2:4, 11.
8. Leviticus 24:7.
9. Philippians 2:13.
10. Numbers 13:33.
11. Romans 8:29.
12. Hebrews 11:6.
13. 1 John 5:10.
14. Hebrews 6:19.

15. James 1:7, 8.
16. 2 Corinthians 5:17.
17. Philippians 2:13.

18. Philippians 1:6.
19. Isaiah 46:10.
20. 1 Corinthians 2:16.

PRESSING IN THROUGH INTERCESSION, PART ONE

CHAPTER 7

I recall that first day of pressing in to His presence, sitting at the feet of our Lord, learning to pray. After pouring out my heart in repentance, I was primed to ask God for His help to overcome the problems of my life. Pausing, I remembered it was the Holy Spirit who is to direct my steps.

"Lord, how should I advance now in prayer? Please teach me."

A Vacation Bible School banner from years past came to mind. It read, J.O.Y.—Jesus, Others, Yourself. This simple, but profound message implied that true joy is attained when priorities are ordered as Jesus *first* and other people *second*. Only then is it safe to focus on self. I felt God was calling me to intercede *first* on behalf of others. I complied.

My habit during intercessory prayer had been to start with family members and friends, then advance to the broader circle of humanity. But, in answer to my asking, the Holy Spirit ordered my prayer.

To my surprise, He reversed my typical pattern. I was led to pray for world situations and leaders, the destitute and downtrodden, believers around the world, associates, church family, friends, extended family, close family members, and finally my spouse, J.D. After several weeks of praying like this, I gleaned understanding of why God ordered my prayer in this fashion. I'll share the reason with you in the next chapter, part two of the teaching on this topic.

It's an understatement to say I did not have a good understanding of intercessory prayer when I began. My feeble attempts were lackluster. You will recall, I had not yet been prompted to include affirmations during this prayer time. When the PRAISE pattern was fully developed (two weeks later), the inherent power of affirmations carried over to my time of intercessions. As I pleaded God's promises over others, He polished my practice of prayer to a new brilliance.

In this chapter and the next, I'll share a few highlights of what the Lord has taught me about intercessory prayer. Here's a preview of seven key points we will briefly consider.

- Our role as intercessors is part of God's plan to bring blessings from heaven.
- We were created to be co-intercessors with Christ.
- Intercessory prayer is the highest calling to ministry.
- We are conformed to the image of Christ through intercessory prayer.
- Intercessory prayer is our duty as Christians.
- Neglecting the call to intercession could be the chief reason that God's work on earth isn't finished.
- Intercessors have their reward—they are doubly blessed.

When we have completed our closer look at these points, I hope your heart will be stirred to spend seasons in earnest intercession, lifting others before His throne of grace. I pray God renews my zeal for this as well. It is perilous not to practice what you teach—God will judge teachers of His Word more strictly.[1]

The altar of incense

A priest entering into the Holy Place (the first compartment of the sanctuary) would see the table of showbread to his right, the golden candlesticks to his left, and the golden altar of incense at the far end of the chamber, centered directly before the veil (the hanging door) to the innermost compartment—the Most Holy Place or "Holy of Holies," which contained the ark of the testimony.

Everything in the sanctuary was representative of Christ and of God's plan of redemption. As we discussed in chapter 6, the table of showbread and affirmations are connected in type. Bible scholars agree the altar of burnt offering represented Christ's sacrifice for our sins, and the golden altar of incense represented His intercession.

Special incense burned upon the golden altar morning and night. It was a compound of fragrant spices and gums—a unique formula given to Moses by God and required for the golden altar. Pronounced most holy, this special incense was used exclusively in the Holy Place, and for no other purpose.[2] As the sweet spices burned continually with fire taken from the bronze altar of sacrifice, the fragrance permeated the Holy Place.

In the early days of the sanctuary services, Aaron, the high priest, burned this incense upon the golden altar.[3] Later, the Levite priests assumed the responsibility—chosen weekly by the casting of lots (a way of determining God's will).[4]

The perfumed smoke rising from the burning incense in front of the veil was an emblem of prayer and a representation of Christ's continual intercession for us:

> Let my prayer be set before You as incense,
> The lifting up of my hands as the evening sacrifice
> *(Psalm 141:2).*

> Now when He had taken the scroll, the four living creatures and the
> twenty-four elders fell down before the Lamb, each having a harp,
> and golden bowls full of incense, which are the prayers of the saints
> *(Revelation 5:8).*

> Then another angel, having a golden censer, came and stood at the altar.
> He was *given* much *incense,* that he should *offer* it *with*
> the prayers of all the saints upon the golden altar which was before the
> throne
> *(Revelation 8:3; emphasis added).*

Please note that a *special* incense—the incense mentioned in Revelation 8:3—is added to and offered with the saints' prayers when they reach the throne room of God. (The word *saint* means "set apart for God" and is applied to all of God's people in both the Old and New Testaments.[5] If you believe in Christ as your Savior, conform to His will, and walk in obedience to Him, you are one of the saints to whom this refers!)

As we exhale the aroma of our prayers, Christ adds His prayers to ours to give them the perfumed fragrance that is pleasing to our Father. His most holy "incense," added in heaven, is the *required* ingredient of God's special formula. It is presented with the offering of the Lamb of God at Calvary's cross—as portrayed by the prescribed fire from the altar of burnt offering.

Only through Christ can our prayers have efficacy. His intercession results in the release of God's blessing. There is one Mediator[6]—One who stands as our Advocate with the Father[7]—Jesus Christ. He alone can make our prayers acceptable, and it is in His name only that we must pray.

Christ, our great Intercessor, pleads for the perishing before God on the merits of what He accomplished at the Cross.

> He was wounded for our transgressions,
> He was bruised for our iniquities;
> The chastisement for our peace was upon Him,
> And by His stripes we are healed. . . .
> Because He poured out His soul unto death,
> And He was numbered with the transgressors,
> And He bore the sin of many,
> And *made intercession* for the transgressors
> *(Isaiah 53:5–12; emphasis added).*

To His disciples, Christ assigns the duty and grants the privilege of intercessory prayer—not because of *our* merits, but on the grounds of trusting in the One who died for our sins, lives to make intercession for us, and is able to save to the uttermost.[8]

Our prayers are acceptable to God because of Christ's intercession. We are instructed to ask in His name, which pleads His intercession.

> And whatever you ask in My name, that I will do, that the Father
> may be glorified in the Son. If you ask anything *in My name,* I will do it
> *(John 14:13, 14; emphasis added).*

You did not choose Me, but I chose you and appointed you that you

> should go and bear fruit, and that your fruit should remain,
> that whatever you ask the Father *in My name* He may give you
> *(John 15:16; emphasis added).*

The Holy Spirit teaches us to pray.[9] Christ's intercession makes it possible for our prayers to be answered!

A temple note

Before we advance in this teaching, let me share an interesting and related note about the temple that stood during Jesus' day. Herod the Great, king of Judea, built this temple, restoring it to the former glory of Solomon's temple in an attempt to gain favor with the Jews.

M. G. Easton's *Illustrated Dictionary of the Bible* contains a drawing of the layout of Herod's temple. Depicted in the outer court were "the place of slaughtering" and the "laver." Between the outer court and the Holy Place is a portico (a sort of open entryway porch). Three doors are labeled—the first, leading to the portico, as "Door called 'The Life' "; the second, leading to the Holy Place as "Door called 'The Truth' "; and the third, to the Holy of Holies, is labeled as "Door called 'The Way.' "

Gazing on this glorious temple, Jesus said, "Do you not see all these things? Assuredly, I say to you, not one stone shall be left here upon another, that shall not be thrown down" *(Matthew 24:2).* True to His prophecy, Roman legions ransacked this temple in A.D. 70. It was utterly destroyed and never rebuilt. The summit of Mount Moriah, where the temple once stood, is now occupied by a mosque, the famous Dome of the Rock.

There is no need for an earthly edifice to serve as God's temple now. The sacrificial system of the Old Covenant came to an end on the day Jesus offered up Himself "once for all."[10] When Jesus died, the ultimate sacrifice was made to atone for the sins of humanity. Christ became our eternal High Priest.[11] All genuine believers become members of His royal priesthood.[12]

"Then the temple of God was opened in heaven, and the ark of His covenant was seen in His temple" *(Revelation 11:19).* God's throne of grace is in His heavenly temple. The earthly temple was a mere copy of the heavenly, made "according to the pattern" God showed Moses on Mount Sinai.[13]

"Do you not know that your body is the temple of the Holy Spirit who is in you, whom you have from God, and you are not your own? For you were bought at a price; therefore glorify God in your body and in your spirit, which are God's" *(1 Corinthians 6:19, 20)*. Now, on earth, God's Spirit abides in living temples—Christ's disciples.

I submit that we also are copies made according to the pattern shown on the mount. It is not Mount Sinai to which I refer, but the mount of Calvary, where our true Pattern—Jesus Christ—revealed the summit of self-sacrificing love. As He is, so must we be in this world.[14]

God has no desire and no need for any other earthly temple. In fact, the book of Revelation discloses at the end of time, when the Holy City—the New Jerusalem—descends from heaven to the re-created earth,[15] there will be no temple in it. Our Almighty God and the His sacrificed Son are its temple.[16]

Jesus said, "I am the way, the truth, and the life. No one comes to the Father except through Me" *(John 14:6)*. "I am the door. If anyone enters by Me, he will be saved" *(John 10:9)*. Man labeled the three doors of Herod's temple, the *life,* the *truth,* and the *way.* Only one "door"—Jesus Christ—is necessary to gain access to God today!

As we press in to God's presence in His heavenly temple, we enter in the name of Jesus, our Door to life and truth. He is the new and living way to approach our Holy God.[17]

Pleading for the perishing

When we intercede for others, we symbolically stand in the Holy Place before the throne of our King. Here we enter into an entirely different sphere of prayer. We reach a higher plane—a place that is very near the heart of Christ.

> In the beginning [before all time] was the Word (Christ),
> and the Word was with God, and the Word was God Himself. . . .
> And the Word (Christ) became flesh (human, incarnate) and
> tabernacled (fixed His tent of flesh, lived awhile) among us
> *(John 1:1–14, AMP).*

For we do not have a High Priest who cannot sympathize

> with our weaknesses, but was in all points tempted
> as we are, yet without sin
> *(Hebrews 4:15).*

Christ became flesh that He might become our perfect Sacrifice, understand our every weakness, and sympathize with us as our great Intercessor before God! To offer us the gift of salvation, He humbled Himself even lower than the angels, and to a humiliating, agonizing death on the cross.[18]

Evangelist Kenneth Cox explains it this way: In God's present order of created beings, there are first of all angels, then man, animals, and finally, insects. He compares Christ's incarnation as a man (a level lower than angels), to a human becoming an insect (a level lower than animals).

As a human being, can you imagine loving an insect enough to humble yourself and become a bug—just so you could intercede for them? Thank God He doesn't ask us to! He simply invites us to open our hearts to the world's lost and suffering souls, and to boldly lift them in prayer before His throne of grace.[19]

The word *intercede* means "to plead or make petition for another." The word *perishing* describes someone who has a loss of well-being, or is in a state of ruin or destruction. I refer to intercessory prayer as "pleading for the perishing."

> Therefore I exhort first of all that . . . *intercessions,*
> and giving of thanks be made for *all* men, for kings
> and all who are in authority. . . . For this is good
> and acceptable in the sight of God our Savior, who desires
> all men to be saved and to come to the knowledge of the truth
> *(1 Timothy 2:1–4; emphasis added).*

From the Bible, the Greek word for "intercessions" is *enteuxis.* It is a technical term for approaching a king, to meet and converse with him by bringing a petition before him, to plead on someone's behalf. As we are pressing more closely in to His presence, this portion of prayer represents acting as a spokesperson for others in a hearing with the King of kings.

Take the helmet of salvation, and the sword of the Spirit,
which is the word of God; praying always with all prayer
and supplication in the Spirit, being watchful to this end
with all perseverance and supplication for *all the saints*
(Ephesians 6:17, 18; emphasis added).

In assurance of salvation and armed with the sword of the Spirit, we are to pray especially for our brothers and sisters in Christ. Still, Paul's exhortation to Timothy applies to us. We are not to limit our prayers only to fellow Christians, but should pray for *all*, even men of authority. To realize that Nero—the heathen enemy who persecuted Christians—was in office at the time Paul wrote this instruction in 1 Timothy makes it more stunning. Obviously, we don't have to agree with a person's political undertakings or approve of his moral standards to pray for him.

Why pray for all? There is only one God, the God of all humankind, and one Mediator, Christ Jesus who died for all. God our Savior "desires all men to be saved and to come to the knowledge of the truth."

Paul had the same heart for the lost. He held intercessors in high esteem, referring to Epaphras—who prayed with the same intensity as Elijah—as "our dear fellow servant" and "a faithful minister of Christ."[20]

Epaphras, who is one of you, a bondservant of Christ, greets you,
always *laboring fervently for you in prayers,*
that you may stand perfect and complete in all the will of God.
For I bear him witness that he has a great zeal for you
(Colossians 4:12, 13; emphasis added).

The effective, fervent prayer of a righteous man avails much.
Elijah was a man with a nature like ours, and he *prayed earnestly*
that it would not rain; and it did not rain on the land
for three years and six months
(James 5:16, 17; emphasis added).

Elijah prayed "earnestly." Literally translated, "he prayed with prayer" or "in praying, he prayed." Epaphras was always "laboring fervently," meaning to strive as in the agony of a contest. In other words, there was nothing casual about their coming before the Lord.

These men who prayed with the great energy supplied by the Holy Spirit are examples for us in intercessions. Theirs were not cold, lifeless, faithless prayers. It was not their eloquence or fervor in which they trusted. It was God! The prayers of the righteous have great efficacy—they are powerful and productive.

God's mercy and loving-kindness are poured out in proportion to our waiting and hoping in Him.[21] Prayer is the key, given by God to man, to open and shut the blessings of heaven!

3ABN's Remnant Prayer Intercessors are a group who intercede in the spirit of Elijah and Epaphras. To date, over fifteen hundred saints worldwide (some representing groups of more than one hundred intercessors) participate in this ministry. When prayer needs are phoned in or e-mailed to 3ABN's pastoral department, they can—by request—be added to this group's prayer list. God has stretched forth His hand to perform signs and wonders in answer to these who labor fervently in intercessory prayer, pleading God's promises.

I encourage you to put Scripture to use as you intercede for others. Returning God's Word to Him in this manner makes us watchmen upon the wall:

> I have set watchmen upon your walls, O Jerusalem,
>   who will never hold their peace day or night;
>   you who [are His servants and by your prayers]
>   put the Lord in remembrance [of His promises],
>   keep not silence, and give Him no rest until
> He establishes Jerusalem and makes her a praise in the earth
> *(Isaiah 62:6, 7, AMP).*

We are to do what is within our power to help humankind, and become a praying people who present others' needs before God's throne. Christ's entire earthly ministry was spent interceding for others, either by action or prayer. He calls us to walk in His footsteps.

Prayer pipeline of blessings

The apparent paradox of prayer is that Christ tells us God knows what we need in advance of our asking,[22] yet He instructs us to ask. This is one of those "higher" thoughts and ways[23] of our Lord. It is, on the surface, perplexing.

> "Ask, and it will be given to you; seek, and you will find; knock, and it will be opened to you. For everyone who asks receives, and he who seeks finds, and to him who knocks it will be opened. Or what man is there among you who, if his son asks for bread, will give him a stone? . . . If you then, being evil, know how to give good gifts to your children, *how much more will your Father who is in heaven give good things to those who ask Him!"* (Matthew 7:7–11; emphasis added).

"You do not have because you do not ask" *(James 4:2).* If God knows what we need *before* we ask, why should we ask?

It is God's will that the work He does on earth through His Holy Spirit is in direct response to the prayers of His people. Prayer is part of Heaven's plan to bring blessings to earth. God does not force His gifts upon us. Infinite wisdom knew that love and loyalty could not be coerced, so He created us as agents of free will and instructs us to choose His gifts through the channel of prayer.

> Prayer is part of Heaven's plan to bring blessings to earth. God does not force His gifts upon us.

To prevent His possible interference with the freedom of choice bestowed upon us, our all-holy, all-loving, all-powerful God waits on us to ask. It is as if God has placed handcuffs of love upon Himself and is waiting for our permission to act.

You may have someone you love who refuses to pray. Many are in this mindset. Your intercession gives God permission to act in their life. Intercessory prayer is the key that unlocks the restraints God has placed upon His own hands to move.

Pressing in to His Presence

I'll share the story of my sister, Sunny, by her permission. Although she was brought up in church, life was not kind to her. To numb her pain, she became a hard-core addict, shooting heroin for many years. I prayed earnestly, begging for God's hand of protection over Sunny and asking Him to send Christian workers across her path—even angels "unawares" if that is what it would take.[24]

I pleaded God's promises over her life:

Cut her free from the cords of the wicked that bind her, O Lord. Open her eyes and turn her from darkness to light. Turn her from the power of Satan to You, that she may receive forgiveness of sins and an inheritance among those who are sanctified by faith in Christ. Please, pour out Your Spirit on her, Lord. Fill her with the Holy Spirit, and by His power put to death the misdeeds of her flesh.[25]

For fifteen years, I agonized over Sunny in prayer. Finally, God got her attention. The rest of her story unfolds like the parable of the prodigal son found in Luke 15:18–23. She returned to the Lord, buried her head into His bosom in deep repentance, and confessed she was undeserving of His love.

God was waiting for her! He gave her His kiss of love, placed the robe of Christ's righteousness around her, put the signet ring of His promises on her finger, and fitted her feet with sandals to press forward on His path of life. The angels in heaven rejoiced.[26] Sunny has been dining from the Lord's table ever since.

"Therefore if the Son makes you free, you shall be free indeed" *(John 8:36)*. Sunny asked to be filled with the Spirit, and by His power she was instantly healed of her destructive addiction. She has remained free for twenty years and has an intimate relationship with the Lord! Glory to God!

You may have heard the testimony of someone who said, "Thank God for a praying mother! Her prayers saved me!" I understand the sentiment, but want to stress our prayers don't *save* anyone. That is God's job. He is very good at it! When loved ones are infected by sin, only the love of God and the blood of Jesus can cure their condition. The Lord desires to receive them for healing, but it is their choice to turn toward Him.

I say this to relieve you of any burden of guilt you might feel when someone for whom you are praying does not turn to be healed by the Lord. God doesn't force His will upon them, and neither can we. However, our prayers do have a significant impact, as they give God permission to work in the life of someone who is rejecting His goodness. After all these years of walking free, Sunny still calls me periodically to give thanks for my prayers. She knows they made a difference.

God longs to bless people!

All prayer—including affirmations from Scripture—is a request. We do not put forth demands for God to fulfill His promises. Often, our human sympathies desire to see immediate temporal relief for suffering souls, without consideration of the eternal outcome. Don't become impatient! When the Lord's answer to prayer is delayed, or perhaps is "No," stand on the foundation of trust in His perfect love and infinite wisdom. Suffering can sometimes serve as the catalyst that turns people to God or strengthens their endurance.

God longs to bless people! He sees the end from the beginning—we see only partially. In 1997, I learned a valuable lesson about asking for God's will when Debbie, a friend from my previous church home, called me in a panic.

"Lisa is in the hospital, and she's dying! Please come and pray for her healing!"

Lisa (not her real name) was Debbie's baby sister, only thirty-two years old. She was more like a daughter to Debbie than a sister.

I dressed hurriedly and drove two hundred miles to the hospital, praying affirmations from Scripture the entire way. Armed with the sword of the Spirit,[27] I stepped from the hospital elevator and rushed to her room. God was with me—I could sense His presence.

Having difficulty breathing, Lisa's mouth formed a slight smile when I leaned down to kiss her forehead. She whispered a greeting, and after a few pleasantries, I was ready to release the power of God's promises in prayer, fully expecting a healing. God had proven to me that He is still in the miracle-working business—I had seen Him raise the sick from their beds in answer to prayer before.

Unexpectedly, the Lord stopped me. I was impressed He had a private message that must first be delivered to Debbie.

"Debbie, God has something He wants to tell you before we pray for Lisa," I said hesitantly after we stepped outside the room. Her tear-filled eyes widened with concern.

"What is it?"

Please, Lord, what do You want me to say to her? I had no idea! There was no still, small Voice this time—I just opened my mouth, and words came flowing out.

"He wants you to know that He loves Lisa even more than you do. He will do what is best for her eternal benefit. If there is any chance that she would turn her back on Him again should He heal her, He wants you to understand that He loves her too much to heal her now and lose her for eternity. Debbie, God wants you to trust His heart!"

Lisa had spent her youth in wild partying and revelry. When first diagnosed with cancer, she surrendered to the Lord's love. Each time the church doors opened, she was there. Her angelic voice could be heard from the choir loft, and she became active in youth ministries. The whole church celebrated when her cancer went into remission and Lisa married. Tragically, it wasn't long afterward that she again rejected God. Three years later, the cancer made a comeback, and Lisa returned to the Lord wholeheartedly.

In the hospital hallway, God's words from Ezekiel 18:21–32 came to my remembrance. He warns that when the righteous turn away from Him, they will suffer spiritual death. But, when the wicked forsake their wicked ways and turn to Him, God will preserve their eternal life. I believed the Holy Spirit had spoken through me.

Grasping Debbie's hand, I prayed, "Lord, please! We ask that Lisa not die one day sooner than Your perfect will, or live one day longer than Your perfect will. We trust Your gracious mercy and Your plan for her life."

Returning to Lisa's bedside, I pleaded all of God's healing promises in prayer. My responsibility was to pray according to His Word and His will. My faith was in God's power, mercy, goodness, and infinite wisdom. The outcome was in His hands.

"Precious in the sight of the LORD is the death of His saints" *(Psalm 116:15)*. Several nights later, Lisa phoned Debbie at home during the middle of the night. In a raspy but excited voice, she shared how God had spoken with her, assuring her of salvation and eventual perfect healing. She told Debbie to quit worrying about her—she was in God's hands. Lisa died that night. A nurse informed the family that she had pulled the breathing tube from her throat. I guess she knew her perfect healing would come in heaven.

Debbie took Lisa's death very hard. A year later she called to thank me for sharing "words straight from the throne of God" on that day outside Lisa's hospital room. The words the Holy Spirit had prompted me to share kept Debbie from sinking too low. God proved to be the Lifter of her head, according to His promise in Psalm 3:3. He had cupped His loving hand under her chin and kept her looking up to Him.

In September of 2008, while we were traveling on ministry business, my precious J.D. had a recurring episode of a mysterious illness. Admitted to the hospital through the emergency room, he required immediate surgery. In the days following, the infectious-disease specialist frequently reminded me of the life-threatening nature of my husband's condition. I was perfectly aware, as it had nearly taken his life twice in the past.

"I have never been closer to the Lord," J.D. told his brother over the phone. "If it's my time to go, I'm ready."

His words sent a chill down my spine. He might be ready, but I was not, and I certainly didn't want him to give up. Striving to remain strong, I efficiently tended to the tasks at hand with robotic action and numbed emotion. For the first eight days, I sat next to his hospital bed, praying constantly in little spiritual gasps, claiming Bible promises for his healing. I dared not press in to God's presence. Each time I tried, I could feel the retaining wall to my emotions begin to give way. I had to maintain my composure for J.D.'s benefit.

"J.D. is too special to God and doing too great a work for the Lord to allow him to die. God is not through with him yet, so have faith and don't worry!" said one dear friend over the phone. A chorus of well-meaning saints chimed in with the same refrain day by day.

I wasn't at all sure they were right. I had recently been ministering to a pastor's wife whose husband had died, seemingly too early in life. He had been doing a great work for the Lord, but now he was gone. I couldn't picture life without J.D., although I morbidly tried. I wanted my husband's perfect healing to take place here and now, not later in heaven.

Ironically, on the day J.D. became ill, I had been delivering a series on faith at the church where I was speaking. Now I questioned my own. Weighing this in my mind, I concluded that concern over the possible death of a loved one is a natural protective instinct, not lack of faith.

Late one night, alone in my hotel room, I finally pressed in to God. The dam broke. Flooded by emotion, I wept openly, pleading for J.D.'s life. A sudden calm came over me.

"Oh, Father, I trust You! I can't see the end from the beginning like You do. If it is Your perfect will that he should die now, I know it is for his eternal benefit. If there is any chance something could interrupt his relationship with You later in life, I plead that You would take him now. If the result of death is not Your perfect will, then I pray in Jesus' name You will restore health unto him. Thank You, Lord." Spending eternity with J.D. was more important than having a few extra years together on earth.

Giving God permission to be God was somehow very settling. It helped me return my focus to Him, trusting in His plan for our lives. That perfect peace that He promises flowed over my raw emotions like a warm, soothing balm.[28] I knew God was in charge, and no matter what happened, He would always be with me.[29] He exchanged His strength for my weakness[30] and carried me in His everlasting arms[31] for the next six months until we passed through the flames of this fiery trial unscorched.[32]

"Why is it that when a child is dying with cancer, God doesn't always answer prayers for healing? Is it because we don't pray with sufficient faith?" my optometrist asked.

It was several weeks ago, while sitting in her examining chair, that I casually mentioned my plan to begin writing a book on prayer. With soulful eyes, this sweet and soft-spoken woman asked if I would explain in the book why some prayers are answered while others are not—especially prayers on behalf of children's lives.

> The righteous perishes,
> And no man takes it to heart;
> Merciful men are taken away,
> While no one considers
> That the righteous is taken away from evil
> *(Isaiah 57:1).*

The devil is a thief who comes only to steal, kill, and destroy.[33] God is the Author of life, and He does not cause a child's illness or death. Why is His answer

"No" to the request for some children's healing? Perhaps He receives them to their rest to avoid evil that could turn them away from Him in their later years or cause unbearable grief.

We cannot see the end from the beginning as God does. We have to trust His heart. This is the best answer I can offer.

What I know with absolute certainty is that God longs to bless us!

Prayer is how we bring down His blessings to earth and to all humankind. He is calling on us to plead for the perishing. We will take a closer look at this duty and privilege in the next chapter, "Pressing in Through Intercession, Part Two."

---

1. James 3:1.
2. Exodus 30:34–38.
3. Exodus 30:8, 9.
4. Luke 1:9–11.
5. Examples: Psalms 116:15; 148:14; Romans 1:7; 15:25; 1 Corinthians 14:33; Jude 14.
6. 1 Timothy 2:5.
7. 1 John 2:1.
8. Hebrews 7:25.
9. Romans 8:26.
10. Hebrews 7:27; 9:26–28; Daniel 9:27.
11. Hebrews 8:1.
12. 1 Peter 2:9.
13. Hebrews 9:24; Exodus 25:40.
14. 1 John 4:17.
15. Revelation 21:2.
16. Revelation 21:22.
17. Hebrews 10:20.
18. Philippians 2:6–8.
19. Hebrews 4:16.
20. Colossians 1:7.
21. Psalm 33:22.
22. Matthew 6:8.
23. Isaiah 55:8, 9.
24. Hebrews 13:2, KJV.
25. Psalm 129:4; Acts 26:18; Romans 8:13, paraphrased.
26. Luke 15:10.
27. Ephesians 6:17.
28. Isaiah 26:3; Philippians 4:7.
29. Hebrews 13:5.
30. Isaiah 40:31; 2 Corinthians 12:9.

Pressing in to His Presence

31. Deuteronomy 33:27.
32. Isaiah 43:1.
33. John 10:10.

Pressing in Through Intercession, Part Two

CHAPTER 8

In part one of this intercessory teaching, we learned that when we intercede for others, we symbolically stand in the Holy Place, before the golden altar of incense. As our prayers rise before the throne of the King of kings, Christ adds His prayers to ours and presents them to the Father. It is His intercession that results in the release of God's blessing.

We observed that pleading for the perishing is accomplished with the great energy supplied by the Holy Spirit. Our approach in prayer is not to be one of casual indifference—we are to pray earnestly and in faith. Still, it is not our eloquence or our fervor in which we are to trust. Rather, we place our trust in God, who longs to bless us and waits on those He created as agents of free will to ask.

Let's review the seven points I promised to present in these two combined chapters:

- Our role as intercessors is part of God's plan to bring blessings from heaven.
- We were created to be co-intercessors with Christ.
- Intercessory prayer is the highest calling to ministry.
- We are conformed to the image of Christ through intercessory prayer.
- Intercessory prayer is our duty as Christians.
- Neglecting the call to intercession could be the chief reason that God's work on earth isn't finished.
- Intercessors have their reward—they are doubly blessed.

Pressing in to His Presence

So far, we have examined our role as intercessors and why it is part of God's plan to bring blessings from heaven. Now we will briefly consider the remaining points.

Created and equipped for intercession

Human beings were created in the image of God. That holy image was marred in humankind after Adam's and Eve's fall to temptation in the Garden of Eden,[1] but God was ready to rescue and re-create the human species through His Calvary plan, and the indescribable gift of salvation.[2] When we accept Christ as our Savior, we are born again—*re-created* in His image!

"The earth is the LORD's, and all its fullness, the world and those who dwell therein" *(Psalm 24:1).* God is the rightful Owner of the earth, but Jesus explains in the parable of the vineyard found in Matthew 21:33–40 that our heavenly Father has "leased" the earth to us and given it over to humankind for development.

> May you be blessed by the LORD,
> Who made heaven and earth.
> The heaven, even the heavens, are the LORD's;
> But the earth He has given to the children of men
> *(Psalm 115:15, 16).*

God made humankind in His image to be co-laborers with Him on the earth—giving us stewardship over this planet. His completed creation of earth contained the full potential for people to develop computers, space shuttles, and iPhones. The Creator gave people creative talents, commanding them to work six days and rest on the seventh—the holy Sabbath.[3]

As God's *re-created* children, our destiny is to become like Christ.[4] When we were adopted by our heavenly Father, we became more than faithful co-laborers with the Lord, we became co-heirs with Christ.[5] Our share in His inheritance carries fundamental responsibilities of the family business.[6] God works to save souls, and we must be about our Father's business until Christ returns.[7] We are "ambassadors for Christ," co-laborers in the spreading of the gospel, entrusted with the "ministry of reconciliation."[8]

We were also re-created to be co-intercessors with Christ, who serves as our great Intercessor in heaven.[9] Our duty as children of God is to participate in the family business by making "intercessions . . . for all men"[10] and to "continue earnestly in prayer" with vigilance.[11]

Prayers of godly intercessors fill the Bible. I think of Abraham, Daniel, and Paul, to name just a few who labored fervently in prayer for humanity. But, intercessory prayer is not consigned to a few special servants of the Lord—it is the duty and great privilege of all of God's children.

"Seek the peace of the city where I have caused you to be carried away captive, and pray to the LORD for it; for in its peace you will have peace" *(Jeremiah 29:7)*. When the people of God were carried away as captives from Jerusalem to Babylon, He instructed them to make a pleasant life there and have children to increase their numbers. God exhorted the captives to intercede on behalf of Babylon.

> Our duty as children of God is to participate in the family business by making "intercessions . . . for all men."

The eyes of the Lord should not have to roam the earth in search of someone who will intercede for a land filled with sinners. Yet, listen to the sorrowful accent in the words of the Lord.

"The people of the land have used oppressions, committed robbery, and mistreated the poor and needy; and they wrongfully oppress the stranger.
So I sought for a man among them who would make a wall,
and stand in the gap before Me on behalf of the land,
that I should not destroy it; but I found no one.
Therefore I have poured out My indignation on them;
I have consumed them with the fire of My wrath;
and I have recompensed their deeds on their own heads,"
says the Lord GOD
(Ezekiel 22:29–31; emphasis added).

> Justice is turned back,
> And righteousness stands afar off;
> For truth is fallen in the street,
> And equity cannot enter.
> So truth fails,
> And he who departs from evil makes himself a prey.
> Then the LORD saw it, and it displeased Him
> That there was no justice.
> *He saw that there was no man,*
> *And wondered that there was no intercessor*
> *(Isaiah 59:14–16; emphasis added).*

God *wondered*—He was amazed that there was no man to intercede! He wondered why no one loved the people enough to intercede. He wondered that no one had faith in His power to deliver.

Is God searching in amazement for intercessors today? Is His holy heart filled with woeful wonder as He searches for someone to "stand in the gap"? I pray not! I pray we will take seriously His call to intercede on behalf of others. Let our hearts understand we are sinning against the Lord when we do not carry out our duty as co-intercessors with Christ.

> Moreover, as for me, far be it from me
> that I should sin against the LORD
> in ceasing to pray for you
> *(1 Samuel 12:23).*

The highest calling

A precious, ninety-three-year-old saint called me at 3ABN. My managerial duties in program development don't normally permit me the leisure of taking such calls, but this was a divine appointment. She encouraged me on a day that I needed it, and I encouraged her.

Sharing stories of her once-active ministerial life, she finally told me of her present homebound condition.

"I'm of no use to my Lord any longer. It depresses me," she sighed.

When I asked how she spent her time, she described her prayer efforts for others throughout the entire day.

"Congratulations," I said. "You have graduated to ministry's highest level! When Christ hands out His rewards, I believe He will call on you to step forth before many of the televangelists. Can't you just see the expressions on their faces?"

It was evident my comments shocked her. In further explanation, I told her that I was convinced intercessory prayer is the highest calling to ministry that exists. Why? Because it is the ministry of our risen and exalted Savior!

> But He, because He continues forever, has an unchangeable
> priesthood. Therefore He is also able to save to the uttermost
> those who come to God through Him, since
> He always *lives to make intercession* for them
> *(Hebrews 7:24, 25; emphasis added).*

> My little children, I write you these things so that you may
> not violate God's law and sin. But if anyone should sin, we have
> an Advocate (One Who will intercede for us) with the Father—
> [it is] Jesus Christ [the all] righteous [upright, just, Who conforms
> to the Father's will in every purpose, thought, and action]
> *(1 John 2:1, AMP).*

> Who is he who condemns? It is Christ who died, and
> furthermore is also risen, who is even at the right hand of God,
> who also makes intercession for us
> *(Romans 8:34).*

The risen and exalted Christ lives to pray for His people! It is because He died for our sins and rose to return to the Father that He now can exercise His right of becoming our Advocate, and ever live to make intercession for us. Our greatest safeguard is that He is alive and constantly interceding on our behalf.

His glorious intercession is the highest expression of ministry, and He invites us to be His prayer partners. Take a moment and think about this. Could there be a higher calling to ministry? Of course, action is vital, but no matter what deeds we do on behalf of His cause, we should always accompany our action with seasons of intercession to release God's power for those we serve.

Sometimes we wonder why—if Christ is interceding on our behalf—our prayers have not seemed to have been answered. Often, because He sees the end from the beginning,[12] He actually *has* answered, and His answer was "No!" I can certainly look back in my life and thank God for what I once considered "unanswered prayers." There are times when His answer is "No" because we have asked with the wrong purpose or selfish motives.[13] At other times His answer is, "Not right now!" God's timing is perfect, and we must learn to trust His wisdom.

Our destiny is to become just like Jesus!

An interesting variation in the timing of answered prayer is presented in the Old Testament book of Daniel. On one occasion, Daniel received an answer while he was still praying.[14] In sharp contrast, the response to another prayer did not arrive until he had fasted and prayed for twenty-one days. The angel delivering God's reply to Daniel assured him that his words had been heard from the moment he began to pray, and explained that a spiritual battle waged in the unseen realms caused the delayed answer.[15]

Christ's ministry of intercession is always potent and productive. We should frequently remind ourselves that God is working all things together for our eternal benefit—to conform us to the image of His Son.[16] I repeat myself; our destiny is to become just like Jesus!

A heart filled with intercession is Christlike. As we pray with the mind and heart of Christ, we become like Him. To pray unceasingly for the perishing world is to resemble Christ's life—our relationship to humankind becomes more like His during these times in prayer.

Intercession is our premier privilege, our highest calling to ministry, and the greatest school of training to become Christlike. The intercessor holds a place of infinite importance in the kingdom of God's grace. God has bestowed this powerful ministry upon us for His work in the salvation of men and the glory of His name.

Unfinished work

To witness an amazing Christlike intercessor's heart in action, just consider Moses. On behalf of a rebellious people, he pleaded with God, "Yet now, if You will forgive their sin—but if not, I pray, blot me out of Your book which You have written" *(Exodus 32:32).*

I confess, I'm not there yet. God still has a work to do in my heart before I would willingly ask Him to remove my name from His book of life[17] to save someone else. I need His divine assistance to become more Christlike, to walk in absolute surrender and live in perfect self-sacrificing love. The time I dedicate to intercessory prayer is unsatisfactory—there is an unfinished work in my heart.

A viewer called 3ABN to level a complaint against me, criticizing a message I had delivered on prayer. She accused me of acting superior and trying to "guilt people into praying more." You might find it interesting to know I had confessed my own need for intensified prayer efforts on the program in question.

I hope you don't feel I am trying to "guilt" you into increased prayer. I believe the message of this chapter—indeed, the message of this book—echoes a wake-up call from God to us, His drowsy church. Christ desires to come soon for His bride, and the bride must be prepared.

Our lack of prayer limits God's work in our lives. Are we likewise limiting His work on earth? Neglecting our calling to intercessory prayer could be the chief reason the work isn't finished. Let me share a story that will illustrate what I mean.

In 2008, I was introduced to Dr. Paul Ratsara, president of the Southern Africa-Indian Ocean Division of the Seventh-day Adventist Church. Within an hour of conversing with him, I recognized he was a godly man. I say this, not to lift him up, but to acknowledge the presence of God in him.

Dr. Ratsara is a man of earnest prayer, who seeks God's wisdom for matters great and small, spending hours daily communicating with the Lord. Finishing the Lord's work is his passion, and he earnestly pleads with Him for direction.

At our first meeting, he shared how God led him to encourage a tiny church (with a membership of only 273 people) of a particular district in his vast division to make a two-year commitment to prayer and fasting. The results in church growth were jaw-dropping, and I had originally planned to share that inspiring report with you now. However, when he arrived at 3ABN this month (January

2010) for an interview, I presented him the rough draft to check for accuracy, and my plan was thwarted.

"Yes, this is accurate," he said, after reviewing my narrative. "But, I think it best that we do not put this in your book. You see, it is a very poor district, and recently the country that shares its border opened. Thousands upon thousands of these church members flooded across to enjoy a better standard of life. We would not want anyone to question the veracity of this report, asking, 'Where are these church members now?' "

I was crestfallen. It was such an incredible report of what the Lord could do through intercessory prayer. I relished writing it.

"I will give you another good report to share," he said with his winsome smile. "This, too, will thrill your heart."

Dr. Ratsara related the story of a devout Muslim who had converted to Christianity and was turning the area in which he lived upside down. A science teacher, his regimented academic schedule interfered with his first love of testifying to God's grace. To increase his time for soul winning, he changed careers. Ironically, he became a farmer, working the fields to support his family and laboring ever more fervently in the harvest fields of the Lord—sometimes conducting up to eight evangelist series a year.

In the first twenty-seven years of his "harvesting" business, this farmer studied his Bible, fasted and prayed, and went forth preaching the Word of God. His harvest was plentiful. He baptized 24,650 people—half of whom were won to Christ during the last seven years! As a result of his ministry, fifty-six churches were planted.

In recent years, the farmer has intensified his time of prayer and fasting up to seven hours daily before, during, and even after his evangelistic campaigns. He earnestly intercedes for the people and makes supplication for the Spirit's power to preach. The great success God has granted him in converting hostile, non-Christians to our Lord has made him unpopular with certain people in this district. Enraged, some plotted and poisoned him. After he ingested the lethal dose (administered by a trusted, but coerced assistant), the Lord miraculously delivered him from death. Later a small group, bonded by mutual hatred, framed him for murder.

"Lord," he cried, "I will not stop praying until You vindicate Your name."

Within three days, the body of the murder victim—weighted with a sixty-six-pound stone to prevent it from floating—was discovered as it surfaced in the river with the massive rock still attached at the waist. Under cross-examination, his false accusers broke down and confessed to the killing. God vindicated His holy name and the farmer's as well.

Most recently, our beloved brother in the Lord conducted a four-week evangelistic series in a small town that had only eighty church members, in an area that is extremely hostile to Christianity. This report reads like a chapter from the book of Acts! Through this farmer, strong in the Spirit from weeks of fasting and praying, the power of God was manifested in an evangelism explosion!

> Most assuredly, I say to you, he who believes in Me,
> the works that I do he will do also; and greater works
> than these he will do, because I go to My Father
> *(John 14:12).*

At the conclusion of the four-week campaign, 3,010 people were baptized! Our dear brother was not interested in posting numbers for the appearance of success. He postponed a good number of other baptisms until those candidates could finish preparation classes and understand with certainty the commitment they were making. Embracing the "Fishers of Men" program (which I'll explain a bit later), these newly baptized Christians won many souls to Christ in just three months.

Hearing the report, my heart leaped for joy, but landed with a thud. I've heard similar stories coming out of Latin countries. Why isn't this happening in the developed nations, such as the United States, Europe, Australia, and New Zealand?

Oh, how we need to be like this dear farmer and Dr. Ratsara—people who intercede for lost souls, people who seek the Lord for instruction and the power to share the gospel so our Lord can return soon! Why aren't we? Is it complacency, lack of prayer and its accompanying power, or simply fear that we don't know enough to share the good news?

Pressing in to His Presence

> Jesus said . . . , "Follow Me, and I will make you become
> fishers of men." They immediately . . . followed Him
> *(Mark 1:17, 18).*

Reports shared by Dr. Ratsara prove, to my satisfaction, that it is not lack of knowledge which limits our soul winning. Led by the Spirit, he implemented the "Fishers of Men" campaign in his division. Newly baptized converts are trained to share their testimony and faith immediately to win souls.

In June 2009, Dr. Ratsara conducted an evangelistic campaign in Angola that resulted in more than six thousand baptisms. At once, these people were put to work for the Lord, and he announced a special Sabbath in October to baptize the converts won by their witnessing. They were given a Bible, a book entitled *Steps to Christ,* and a few other materials; and after simple training, they were sent forth. They each had a little more than three months to win one soul!

Like the Samaritan woman who encountered Jesus at the well,[18] they went—with the excitement of discovering the Messiah—into their villages to tell others what Christ had done for them. The special baptism was held in October 2009 and resulted in 14,396 more souls being baptized into Christ. Just a matter of months later (December 2009), another 22,850 people were baptized.

At the time of this writing, God has added an increase of at least 37,246 souls (in just six months) through the seed of those original 6,000-plus people baptized in June of 2009 at Dr. Ratsara's campaign. In perfect similitude to the book of Acts, this story has no conclusion!

What would happen if church members around the world woke up to their duty as co-intercessors and co-laborers with Christ? What would happen if we earnestly prayed for the Lord of the harvest to send laborers into His harvest fields?[19] What if we pleaded for God to pour out His Holy Spirit in the latter rain?[20]

The answer to these questions finds a witness in the personal stories of those 273 church members, the farmer, the "fishers of men," and our dear brother, Dr. Ratsara. Fervent prayer would bring about greater workings of the Holy Spirit in our churches and our individual lives if we would be like those who patterned their lives after Elijah and earnestly prayed—praying with prayer.

A double-portion blessing

My husband is the kind of man who knows how to make everyone feel special. J.D. is never too hurried to acknowledge each and every person around him, taking time to uplift them in conversation.

When we attend events, he frequently tells me in advance we should plan on leaving at a certain hour. At the designated time I dutifully head for the door, appearing anxious to leave, only to wait while he circles the room on his goodbye tour—capping off the occasion with words of encouragement to everyone. Sometimes these tours are quite lengthy. If anyone shares a problem or concern, J.D. immediately prays with them.

I try to respond in the same manner, but sometimes fall short on my efforts. It seems I am destined to rush from one deadline to another (perhaps a destiny of my own making). I'm geared to bolt off an elevator as soon as the door opens—like a racehorse out of the starting gate— whether we've reached the right floor or not.

Praying for another in their presence is a form of intercessory prayer.

"I'll pray for you!" Have you ever mouthed these words and forgot to carry through? It's best to pray with people immediately when we know they have a need. Praying for another in their presence is a form of intercessory prayer.

When we learn of someone's problems—whether through a firsthand report or discernment—God is inviting us to pray. The personal difficulties of others are not revealed to us so that we may wag our tongues to start a whisper campaign. Gossip is nothing more than Satan's sick counterfeit to intercession.

In my race against time, I don't always pray with someone immediately. In those instances, I ask God to bring their need to my remembrance and cause me to be faithful in prayer. Keeping a prayer list handy would be ideal, but I don't. My prayer journal serves this purpose. I can review my segments on intercessory prayer and be prompted to intercede again for someone who has yet to see an answer.

When I do pray with someone personally, I try to remember afterward to share one piece of advice—"Pray for others who are in your situation." I advise you to do the same. For example, if you have just suffered a divorce, intercede for others who are facing similar emotional strain.

This advice serves a good purpose. Just as praying for the salvation of someone who has hurt you can introduce forgiveness to your heart, interceding for a person in a similar situation to yours can foster patience and endurance in you.

Your double-portion blessing on earth may be spiritual growth and an increased intimacy with God, and in heaven a joy inexpressible.

Often as you sincerely seek God's mercy and comfort for someone else, you will find a greater measure of mercy and comfort for yourself. You are, in a sense, casting your bread upon the waters, and God's Word says it will come back to you.[21] When you give a measure of sympathy and devotion in intercession, God measures it back to you.

"Give, and it will be given to you: good measure, pressed down,
shaken together, and running over will be put into your bosom.
For with the same measure that you use, it will be measured back to you"
(Luke 6:38).

Certainly, avoid praying for others with a selfish motivation of gaining personal benefits. This would displease God, who knows your heart. Still, there is a reward that accompanies intercessory prayer.

Intercessors are doubly blessed!

You are most likely familiar with the story of the ancient patriarch Job. Satan did everything he could to ruin Job's life, including placing an unsympathetic spirit in his friends who were sent to "comfort" Job. After enduring a long-winded dispute with his companions, Job finally turned his eyes toward heaven and interceded on their behalf. Mercy and forgiveness flowed, and God responded by giving Job a double-portion blessing.

The LORD restored Job's losses
when he prayed for his friends. Indeed the LORD
gave Job *twice as much* as he had before
(Job 42:10; emphasis added).

All intercessors may not be flooded with earthly fortunes, but God will multiply His love, mercy, and grace to you. Intercession inspires a living relationship with the Lord. Your double-portion blessing on earth may be spiritual growth and an increased intimacy with God, and in heaven a joy inexpressible.

As we pour out our hearts in the priestly work of intercession, we are pressing in to the heart of Heaven. When we stand in the gap to plead for the perishing—praying God's blessing down on the world—we demonstrate Christ's love for the lost and suffering and our faith in God's power to deliver. God shines His face on us in pleasure and approval.

In chapter 7, the first part of our intercessory teaching, I promised to share why I believe the Holy Spirit directed my prayer in the order He did. Praying for others first certainly squashes self-centeredness, but why did He have me intercede by beginning with the broader circle of humanity, then slowly narrow my focus to those with whom I share a common bond, and finally to focus on my beloved husband?

I believe it was for the purpose of increasing intimacy in prayer before He took me to the next segment. My appeals for world situations, the downtrodden, Christians around the world, and my associates were sincere. Prayers for my church family and friends engendered even greater enthusiasm. At the point of praying for my extended and close family members, I was praying with heartfelt confidence. Ultimately, praying for J.D. aroused intimate and passionate prayer.

God was preparing my heart to be laid bare before Him as I pressed further in to His presence. With open-hearted intimacy, I was ready to make meaningful, honest supplication on behalf of my own life.

---

1. Genesis 3.
2. Revelation 13:8; Ephesians 2:8–10; 2 Corinthians 9:15.
3. Exodus 20:8–11.
4. Romans 8:29.

5. Romans 8:17.
6. Colossians 3:24.
7. John 5:17; Luke 19:24.
8. 2 Corinthians 5:18–20.
9. Hebrews 7:25.
10. 1 Timothy 2:1.
11. Colossians 4:2.
12. Isaiah 46:10.
13. James 4:3.

14. Daniel 9:20–22.
15. Daniel 10:10–13.
16. Romans 8:28, 29.
17. Examples: Revelation 3:5; 20:15; 21:27.
18. John 4:1–41.
19. Luke 10:2.
20. Zechariah 10:1.
21. Ecclesiastes 11:1.

PRESSING IN THROUGH SUPPLICATION

CHAPTER 9

Growing up in an extremely dysfunctional environment, I had no one close to me whom I could really trust. Deeply ingrained in my psyche, from experiences at home and in church, was the sense I had to be perfect to be loved. I adapted by becoming a fiercely independent "take charge" kind of person, who constantly strove to be perfect to gain approval. Society praised me for these attributes, but my orientation toward self-performance kept me from experiencing the power of full surrender to God.

I didn't understand the disadvantage of the burden I tried to carry until God taught me the secret of walking in the power of surrender. This chapter contains that lesson.

In this book I have pointed out, as a matter of observation only, the similarities of the PRAISE prayer pattern to the ancient earthly sanctuary pattern. On the basis of this symbolism, we will consider the last piece of furniture within the Holy Place—the golden candlestick—and my perceived connection with this prayer segment on supplication.

First, let's look at the definition of *supplication* and consider the dual application of this word within Scripture.

Numerous words from original Bible languages refer to an aspect of prayer and are generally translated into English as "prayer, pray, or ask." The word translated as "intercession," is almost exclusively used in reference to praying for others. In contrast, "supplication" is used in Scripture to describe both prayers for others and prayers for self. It means "to make an entreaty"—a cry from the heart—and stresses a sense of need.

When praying for special needs for self in the midst of prayer, the word *supplication* is often put into service.

Hear my *prayer*, O LORD,
Give ear to my *supplications!*
In Your faithfulness answer me,
And in Your righteousness
(Psalm 143:1; emphasis added).

[Jesus], in the days of His flesh, when He had
offered up *prayers and supplications,* with vehement cries
and tears to Him who was able to save Him from death,
and was heard because of His godly fear [reverence]
(Hebrews 5:7; emphasis added).

Be anxious for nothing, but in everything by *prayer and supplication,*
with thanksgiving, let your requests be made known to God
(Philippians 4:6; emphasis added).

David frequently used the word *supplication* as he pleaded for his own benefit. In the Garden of Gethsemane, Christ made supplication for Himself in the midst of His prayers. Paul advises to add thanksgiving with our supplication in prayer.

For the purpose of the PRAISE prayer pattern, *supplication* is used to refer to *prayers on behalf of self.*

Pressing in to His presence, we have already practiced the principles of Praise, Repentance, Affirmations, and Intercession. It's time for Supplication— to come before God, expressing heartfelt needs of our own. With clean hands, a pure heart, and godly reverence, we will come boldly (but humbly) before His throne of grace to make intimate appeals to our heavenly Father for help in our time of need.

Let us therefore come boldly to the throne of grace, that we

may obtain mercy and find grace to help in time of need
(Hebrews 4:16).

The golden candlestick

The sanctuary was a covered tent without windows, so there was no natural light within. The presence of God's Shekinah glory provided brightness in the Holy of Holies, while the golden candlestick was the light bearer in the Holy Place.

The seven-branched candlestick (the "Great Menorah" in Hebrew) was an exquisitely decorated work of art, made according to the divine pattern given by God on Mount Sinai.[1] Approximately five feet tall and constructed of pure gold, it was formed by hand (not poured into a mold).[2] From its base rose a single pillarlike trunk (the lampstand), and six branches came out from sides of the main trunk—three on one side, and three on the other.[3]

Multiple almond-shaped bowls on the trunk and on each of the branches held the purest hand-pressed olive oil as the fuel for the seven richly adorned lamps.[4] The lamps provided necessary light in the Holy Place for the priests to perform their duties, and they burned continually.

> "You shall command the children of Israel that they
> bring you pure oil of pressed olives for the light,
> to cause the lamp to burn continually"
> *(Exodus 27:20).*

Scholars disagree whether the lamp burned both day and night, or during the night only. Several Bible passages are difficult to interpret on this matter. The argument in favor of burning through the night only is based on the requirement of the priests dressing the lamp each morning and necessarily snuffing out the seven flames.

God commands in Exodus 27:20 and Leviticus 24:2 the continual burning of the lamp. To support the position of burning both day and night, the texts which describe dressing the lamp would indicate cleaning one lamp at a time. Common sense supports this interpretation.

The hanging "door" to the entrance[5] of the tabernacle shut out natural light in the thirty-by-fifteen-foot room. If the priests snuffed out all seven lamps simultaneously, how would they see to remove the ashes and replenish the oil? For that matter, how would they see to perform their other priestly duties each day?

I am convinced the scholars who support the continual burning of the lamps are correct, especially as I consider the symbolic representation of the golden candlestick.

So how does the sanctuary symbolism of the golden candlestick relate to us and our time of supplication? In the interest of brevity, I will offer a quick parallel-point summary.

In Revelation 1:11–13, the apostle John describes Christ walking among seven golden lampstands, identified in verse 20 as seven churches of apostolic times (which typified the condition of Christian churches throughout world history).

We are the church! Our bodies are the temple of God, but there is no natural light within us. Jesus is our great Lampstand—the Light of the world, and in Him we have branchlike life.[6] He is actually called the "Branch" in Scripture,[7] and God refers to His people as "the branch of My planting, the work of My hands."[8]

We are God's "workmanship,"[9] re-created in the image of Christ according to the divine pattern shown on the hill of Calvary.[10] God is purifying and refining us by His hand into vessels of pure gold, so that we may present Him offerings in righteousness.[11]

In Bible symbolism, oil represents the Holy Spirit. Kings and priests were anointed with oil, and now that the Holy Spirit has been poured out on us, we have His anointing.[12]

In the book of Revelation, the sevenfold Spirit of God is before His throne.[13] The number seven is the symbolic expression of completion or perfection. It is the power of the sevenfold Holy Spirit that keeps the flame of godly zeal burning in our hearts continually, as represented by the oil that fueled the seven-branched lamps.

> Never lag in zeal and in earnest endeavor; be aglow
> and burning with the Spirit, serving the Lord
> *(Romans 12:11, AMP).*

The priests of old were required to dress the candlestick each morning, throwing out the ashes and refilling the oil. As we go before the Lord with our supplication, I consider that we are symbolically dressing the seven-branched candlestick in the morning. We have previously discarded the ashes through repentance, and now we come seeking a fresh supply of His Spirit.

> Then he said to me, This [addition of the bowl to the candlestick,
> causing it to yield a ceaseless supply of oil from the olive trees]
> is the word of the Lord to Zerubbabel, saying,
> *Not by might, nor by power, but by My Spirit*
> [of Whom the oil is a symbol], says the Lord of hosts
> *(Zechariah 4:6, AMP; emphasis supplied).*

We need God to pour out His "Spirit of grace and supplication."[14] Grace for power to go through the day victoriously, and supplication as guided by the Spirit—for we know not how to pray for ourselves.

> So too the [Holy] Spirit comes to our aid and bears us up
> in our weakness; for we do not know what prayer to offer
> nor how to offer it worthily as we ought, but the Spirit Himself
> goes to meet our supplication and pleads in our behalf with
> unspeakable yearnings and groanings too deep for utterance
> *(Romans 8:26, AMP).*

His desires become your desires

"Delight yourself also in the LORD, and He shall give you the desires of your heart" *(Psalm 37:4)*. What a beautiful promise, and what a tragedy it has been hijacked by prosperity teachers, who twist the Scriptures to their own destruction.[15] These false prophets foster the idea of naming almost anything *you* want, and claiming it from God, saying, "Ye have not, because Ye claim not!" They do not consider the context of their reference or what the rest of Scripture says.

Yet you do not have because you do not ask.

> You ask and do not receive, because you ask amiss,
> that you may spend it on your pleasures
> *(James 4:2–4).*

> Do not love the world or the things in the world.
> If anyone loves the world, the love of the Father is not in him.
> For all that is in the world—the lust of the flesh, the lust of the eyes,
> and the pride of life—is not of the Father but is of the world
> *(1 John 2:15, 16).*

When we find our delight in God, His desires become our desires. Our all-consuming passion is not for a new Mercedes-Benz vehicle; rather, we hunger and thirst for righteousness.[16]

Like Jacob in his mysterious wrestling session of prayer, we cry out, "I will not let You go unless You bless me!"[17] This is the only Bible example I can think of where prayer was presented as a demand rather than a request. And, it *was* prayer, for the Man with whom Jacob wrestled was God.[18] The Lord rewarded him with a change of character—symbolized by changing his name (which meant *deceiver*) to Israel, a *victor with God*!

In my own prayer experience, as God increased the intimacy and intensity of my prayers through pressing in to His presence, I learned to be like Jacob, making supplication first for that which was most important—a changed character. When we delight ourselves in the Lord, we pray for those things which are most important to Him, and He graciously adds our required necessities to our lives.

> Seek first the kingdom of God and His righteousness,
> and all these things shall be added to you
> *(Matthew 6:33).*

Moreover, as we seek His righteousness first, our Father—who longs to bless us—gifts us with many pleasant surprises. Perhaps the greatest example of this principle in action is the account of Solomon's prayer, found in 1 Kings 3. He loved the Lord, but was far from perfect.

God instructed Solomon, "Ask! What shall I give you?" Acknowledging the Lord's goodness, the young king asked for nothing more than wisdom to rule over God's people. This request found favor with the Almighty.

> "Because you have asked this thing, and have not asked
> long life for yourself, nor have asked riches for yourself . . .
> behold, I have done according to your words. . . .
> *And I have also given you what you have not asked:*
> both riches and honor, so that there shall not be anyone
> like you among the kings all your days"
> *(1 Kings 3:11–13; emphasis added).*

Jesus teaches us to pray for our daily needs,[19] so it is scriptural to pray for life's necessities. Still, let me ask a penetrating question. Above and beyond critical requirements, if God spoke to you saying He would give you *anything* you desire, what treasures would be on your list? Priorities can be probed by inspecting the intrinsic values of the things you long for—are they essential for eternity?

God has taught me there is one supreme prayer request I should present first when I come before Him with supplication. The matter of foremost importance, to be desired above all else, is to pray for a continuous filling of the Holy Spirit—the very thing He commands, and what He is most eager to do!

> Ever be filled and stimulated with the [Holy] Spirit
> *(Ephesians 5:18, AMP).*

> "If you then, being evil, know how to give good gifts
> to your children, how much more will your heavenly Father
> give the Holy Spirit to those who ask Him!"
> *(Luke 11:13).*

One of the great desires of our Father's heart is for us to recognize our need to be filled with His Spirit and to walk in surrender to His will. We should ask Him daily for this great gift of grace. I will prove this from Scripture in a moment. For now, we need only to consider why.

If we call ourselves Christians but do not possess the Spirit of God, we are nothing more than pretenders—people who profess to belong to God's family, when, in fact, we have not been born again.[20] We may be convinced, but we are not converted.[21]

The "sentimental Christian" who professes love for Christ, but refuses to walk in obedience, lacks the Spirit of God.[22] The pharisaical "legalistic Christian," devoted to doctrine rather than to Christ, lacks the Spirit of God.[23] Both are walking in the flesh and, *flesh* defined is "the nature of man without the Holy Spirit." Can anyone without the Spirit represent Christ? To God, this is nonsense—to our fellow man, it is a nuisance.

To dress the lamp, we must "put off" the old *flesh* nature and "put on" the *new* nature re-created in the image of Christ.[24] Daily, we should ask to be filled with the Spirit. As we ask and receive from God the gift of His precious Holy Spirit, our carnal soul—once ruled by the base fleshly nature—is subdued by sovereign grace.

> For this reason I bow my knees to the Father of our Lord Jesus Christ . . .
> that *He would grant you,* according to the riches of His glory,
> *to be strengthened with might through His Spirit in the inner man.* . . .
> Now to Him who is able to do exceedingly abundantly above all
> that we ask or think, *according to the power that works in us,*
> to Him be glory in the church by Christ Jesus to all generations
> *(Ephesians 3:14–21; emphasis added).*

There is only one way to walk with God—we must be filled with the Holy Spirit day by day! This is how we possess the life of Christ. His Spirit makes a profound difference in our lives as He works His power to create God's purity and purposes in us.

Oh, may the recognition of our great need bring us to our knees, and may our heart cry of supplication be, "Fill me with Your Spirit, Father!" He is eagerly waiting to respond, and as He does, our hearts will be ablaze with the power and presence of God!

From glory to glory

Sometime late in the year 2000, I experienced a short-term spiritual falter when I quit practicing life affirmations from Scripture for a couple of weeks. Practicing the affirmations was a vital practice that God had taught me to do, and I was *not* doing it. The strong desire I previously had for this practice seemed to be overridden by a type of spiritually numbing resistance. One morning, as I pressed in to His presence, I reached a pivotal point and forced myself to include affirmations in my prayer.

"Thank You, Father, that because I am joined to You, I am one in spirit with You" *(1 Corinthians 6:17, paraphrased)*.

My words of affirmation had a crushing impact. Earlier that year, I had completed a study on the Hebrew word for "one" found in Deuteronomy 6:4. It is a *uniplural* word (the perfect union of multiple components), and means "to be *united* in thought, purpose, and action." I was far from being *one in spirit* with God, but I wanted to be. By faith, I accepted this was God's will for me and that He would work this oneness into my heart if only I would cooperate. I began to weep.

"Please, Father, I know I'm not one with You. I'm simply calling things that are not as though they already were. But, Lord, I don't know *how* to become one with You! Why is it I run in a teaching that You have given me, then awake one day to find I am no longer following it? Please help me understand!"

"I will soon explain to you the wall of resistance *you are hitting,"* the heavenly answer came.

His thought, impressed upon my mind, was stunning. *Exactly! That's it! That's how I feel—like I hit a wall!* Although I did not know the solution to my problem, I was somehow comforted. God understood and would soon share the solution!

For two weeks, I prayed that the Lord would explain the "wall of resistance" I so frequently hit. Each day, my prayers became more earnest. Finally, God answered my plea after yet one more affirmation that engulfed my emotions.

"Thank You, Father, that I am beholding in Your Word, as in a mirror, Your glory—Your character—and that I am being transformed into Your image from glory to glory, from one level of Your character to the next, by the power of Your

Holy Spirit," I boldly confessed, taking from 2 Corinthians 3:18.

My eyes stung hot and sorrow poured forth in tears. I am not a weepy woman, but I felt I was in a spiritual stupor and powerless to advance in my Christian walk. I needed help to get beyond this mysterious wall that blocked my way.

As I was seeking God with solemn, heartrending humility, a scene appeared in my mind. Has that ever happened to you? For lack of a better description, I call them *instructional* prayer visions (like Paul had when he prayed in Acts 9:10–12). I've spoken with many saints who have experienced these little pictorial tutors.

I saw a huge staircase illuminated by a bright light and ascending into the heavens. The staircase had exceedingly high steps—each of which were drawn out a great distance in length, as well. There I was, running along one of the lower steps, glancing back over my shoulder. Without warning, *whack*—I hit a wall!

"What is it, Lord? What is this wall I am hitting?"

"Every time you hit the wall, it is a wall of self-preservation *you hit! You are headed in the right direction, but looking back to self. Turn full-faced to Me, child. Keep your eyes on Me!"*

The Lord caused me to understand what this scene depicted. Each step represented another level of His glory, which is the brightness of His character (as proclaimed to Moses in response to his request to see the glory of God).[25] Each advancing step symbolized achieving another level of the Lord's character.

In my mind, I moved backward from the wall to get a better overview. Looking upward, I realized the wall was actually the front side of the next step. I gasped at the size of it, which was at least ten times taller than my height. I could see no way to climb it.

"How do I get over the wall, Lord? How do I reach the next step?"

"To scale the wall of self-preservation, to become more like Me, you must be willing to give up more of self-interests. You must be willing to surrender to Me. Take My hand, and I will lift you up."

He directed me to a Scripture that has become one of my many favorites.

> For You are my lamp, O Lord;
> The Lord shall enlighten my darkness. . . .
> *By my God I can leap over a wall*
> *(2 Samuel 22:29, 30; emphasis added).*

"The entrance of Your words gives light; it gives understanding to the simple" *(Psalm 119:130)*. I was prompted to study on the topic of becoming more Christ-like. I had already tasted the transforming power of His promises[26] and understood God worked in me to will and to act according to His good pleasure,[27] but achieving His character still seemed mysteriously elusive.

"To them God willed to make known what are the riches of the glory of this mystery . . . which is Christ in you, the hope of glory" *(Colossians 1:27)*. The life of Christ being lived out in me was my only hope of achieving His glory—His character! Further study convinced me that in order to have more of Christ's life in me, I needed more of His Spirit.

We can be *filled* with the Holy Spirit only to the degree we are *emptied* of self. God had impressed me that to make it over the wall of self-preservation, I must come to Him and be willing to surrender—willing to deny self and to be filled with His Spirit. Further, He said that if I took His hand, He would lift me up!

> But we all, with unveiled face, beholding as in a mirror
> the glory of the Lord, are being transformed into the same
> image *from glory to glory*, just as *by the Spirit of the Lord*
> *(2 Corinthians 3:18; emphasis added).*

It was to be a work of the Spirit. All I had to do was surrender. But how?

Walking in the power of surrender

What does the word *surrender* mean to you? Judging by audience's responses I have received over many years of posing this question, I think I can guess. If you are a typical man, you most likely think surrender is a sign of weakness, of giving up—the war is over, and you are being taken captive. If you are a woman, the word *surrender* might send a shudder down your spine, accompanied by visions of someone controlling your every action.

Pressing in to His Presence

Is this along the line of your thinking? For most people it is. Yet we tell the poor worldly soul to whom we are witnessing that all they have to do is surrender to God. How can we better explain this in a way that sounds inviting to their carnal ears? What steps do we offer as instruction?

Several weeks after God identified the obstacle to my Christian advancement as a wall of self-preservation, I still struggled with surrender. Oh, how I desired to fully submit my life to the Lord. I just didn't know the way.

"Thank You, Father, that I abide in Jesus and walk just as He walked" *(1 John 2:6, paraphrased)*. It probably won't surprise you to learn my eyes became wet with tears, as I prayed this affirmation on another morning. Yes, I was calling things that are not as though they were,[28] but it was painful to recognize how little progress I had made, and it caused my faith to wobble. It was time to wrestle with the Lord, as Jacob had.

"Lord, I am returning Your Word. You promised it would not return to You void.[29] You promised to watch over it to perform it![30] Please, Lord, show me how to walk in surrender as Jesus walked. I will not let You go unless You bless me with a changed character![31] Cause me to follow in Christ's footsteps!"

Instantly, in my mind, I saw a gigantic elephant. Next to him was a tiny little sugar ant, hardly visible. *What does this mean?* I wondered.

"Shelley, the greatest strength you can muster is like that of the tiny ant. Whereas My power is, by comparison, like that of the elephant. Why would you want to walk in your limited human strength, when I make My power available to you? When I ask you to surrender, child, I am asking you to accept My power."

Galatians 3:3 came to my remembrance, "Are you so foolish? Having begun in the Spirit, are you now being made perfect by the flesh?" Yes, I had been so foolish. Trying my utmost to walk with God, I had been drawing only on my own sugar-ant strength. It was like that tiny insect trying to roll a boulder up a hill!

Now I realize that each morning of my life, I face a decision that determines whether I walk as a *pitiful* or a *powerful* Christian that day. If I attempt to perfect my walk by the strength of my flesh, I am to be pitied as I limp along, hobbled by self-destructive habits. If I choose to walk in the power of the Spirit, I can run the race of faith with joy.

"But he said to me, 'My grace is sufficient for you, for my power is made perfect in weakness.' Therefore I will boast all the more gladly about my weaknesses, so that Christ's power may rest on me" *(2 Corinthians 12:9, NIV)*. This message, given by Jesus to Paul, was the same that I was now receiving. His grace—His divine assistance and supernatural power unto salvation—was all I needed!

"Father," I cried, "Your Word says in Psalm 16:11 that You will make known to me Your path of life, and cause me to experience joy in Your presence. How do I walk as Jesus walked, in the power of surrender?"

"If you will *to walk like Jesus, you must follow the path of His passion."*

These were the only words the still, small voice of the Lord impressed upon my mind, but it made perfect sense. The gateway to salvation is the Crucifixion. The word *passion* as applied to our Savior, refers to His suffering of the Calvary plan on our behalf.

Immediately I immersed myself in Bible study, determined to learn the mystery of walking in the power of surrender. I wanted to walk like Jesus.

Three steps forward with Christ

Do you ever weary of the old three-steps-forward, two-steps-back routine in your Christian walk? The way to overcome this is to learn to walk in the power of surrender, and it is not that mysterious after all.

"You must follow the path of His passion," was the Spirit's advice, referring to walking as Jesus walked. Three great events along this path caught my interest and highlighted symbolic significance for my quest to surrender.

"He will teach us His ways, and we shall walk in His paths" *(Micah 4:2)*. First, we must come to that place where we are like Jesus in the Garden of Gethsemane. Next, we advance to the point where our actions resemble Christ's with respect to the hill of Calvary. Finally, we embody and celebrate the power of resurrected life, as Jesus did the morning He arose from the tomb.

Let's look at how these steps teach surrender, and look at the Scripture promises we can plant in our hearts to be transformed.

Step 1—In the Garden

"Father . . . not My will, but Yours, be done"
(Luke 22:42).

Pressing in to His Presence

The first step of surrender is to pray as Jesus prayed in the Garden of Gethsemane, asking for God's will to be done rather than ours. When first learning the steps of surrender, I was quite humble in my supplications. One day I became a little full of myself and stepped out ahead of God.

"Lord, I am willing to do Your will!" I boldly stated in prayer.

"No, you are not!"

Startled, and momentarily silenced by His words, I mulled this over. I thought I was willing, but I had an important lesson to learn. If I were truly willing, I would already be walking in perfect obedience to what God had previously taught me, which I was not.

"Oh, Father," I cried. "I'm willing to be made willing!"

"That's all I ask of you."

"For it is God who works in you both to will and to do for His good pleasure" *(Philippians 2:13)*. We need God's power to change our will. For us to be willing, God must first do a work in our hearts. Once that has been achieved, we can step out in faith, knowing that God will infuse us with power to act in a manner pleasing to Him.

"I delight to do Your will, O my God, and Your law is within my heart" *(Psalm 40:8)*. I always pray this when I am seeking to surrender to God. At first, it was spoken in the spirit of faith only—calling things that did not exist as if they did. Let's be honest! Not everything God asks us to do appeals to our natural minds. But, as I prayed this affirmation, God's Word did not return void. He has performed a work in my heart that makes doing His will a delight.

"Teach me to do Your will, for You are my God; Your Spirit is good. Lead me in the land of uprightness" *(Psalm 143:10)*. This cry of David is a powerful supplication that we should include in our prayer of surrender each morning. (Take time to read Psalm 143 in its entirety—it is a superior example of supplication in prayer.)

"Your Teacher will not hide Himself any more, but your eyes will constantly behold your Teacher. And your ears will hear a word behind you, saying, This is the way; walk in it, when you turn to the right hand and when you turn to the left" *(Isaiah 30:20, 21, AMP)*. When we ask God to teach us His will, we can count on His doing just that. Pray to hear the still, small voice of the Lord[32] and to respond to your Teacher.

"Let this mind be in you which was also in Christ Jesus, who . . . made Himself of no reputation. . . . He humbled Himself and became obedient to the point of death, even the death of the cross" *(Philippians 2:5–8)*. Christ loved sinners, but loathed sin. Sin was an abomination to His holy character. We need to pray for the mind of Christ. We must despise sin and desire to avoid it at all costs. There is a cost. To walk in absolute humility like Christ, we must be willing to die to self.

Step 2—On the cross

He said to them all,
"If anyone desires to come after Me,
let him deny himself, and
take up his cross daily,
and follow Me"
(Luke 9:23).

"We've all got our cross to bear." Have you ever heard this saying? Typically it is accompanied by a description of some earthly burdens that don't seem fair. It is a pitiful application of the principal found in Luke 9:23.

"I die daily" *(1 Corinthians 15:31)*. The apostle Paul understood what Jesus meant by taking up his cross daily. In fact, every person to whom Christ spoke knew that to "take up your cross" meant you were on the way to be crucified unto death. The secret of Paul's victorious walk with the Lord is that he understood how to die to self daily and live for God.

I warn you in advance, this step is difficult to consider—it isn't achieved in an instant. We so little understand the principle of dying to self. Earthly things excite the lust of our flesh, the lust of our eyes, and the pride of life, but their pleasures are only passing.[33] To be friends with the world is to be enemies of God—we break our Father's heart.[34] We must set our minds on things above, not on things of the earth.[35] This requires self-denial at every step to walk victoriously with God. Who can do it?

"Can the Ethiopian change his skin or the leopard its spots? Then may you also do good who are accustomed to do evil" *(Jeremiah 13:23)*. We have no better chance of changing our carnal nature by our human strength than the sugar ant has of rolling a boulder up the hill. Don't become discouraged. God knows, and He is waiting for us to draw on His power—that's His plan!

"For if you live according to the flesh you will die; but if *by the Spirit* you put to death the deeds of the body, you will live" *(Romans 8:13; emphasis added)*. When Jesus said to take up our cross daily, He knew we didn't have the power to crucify our own flesh-nature. We need a co-executioner. We need the Holy Spirit!

Notice Romans 8:13 clearly states *by the Spirit* working within us *we* put to death our misdeeds. It's a joint operation. We must cooperate with the Spirit of God, counting on His power. Our heart-cry should be, "Lord, help me pick up my cross and die to self! Cause me, by the power of Your Spirit, to put to death the misdeeds of my flesh."

"Those who are Christ's have crucified the flesh with its passions and desires. If we live in the Spirit, let us also walk in the Spirit" *(Galatians 5:24, 25)*. The only way we can keep in step with the Spirit is if our flesh has been crucified. Only then will we not lag behind Him or run ahead of Him.

"I have been crucified with Christ; it is no longer I who live, but Christ lives in me; and the life which I now live in the flesh I live by faith in the Son of God, who loved me and gave Himself for me" *(Galatians 2:20)*. When Christ lives in us, we enjoy abundant life on earth[36] and receive an inheritance that won't fade away in eternity.[37] That's a life well spent!

"God forbid that I should boast except in the cross of our Lord Jesus Christ, by whom the world has been crucified to me, and I to the world" *(Galatians 6:14)*. Do we find our boast in the Lord's salvation? Is the world crucified to us, or do we still respond to its siren song? What profit is there if we gain the whole world, and lose our own souls?[38]

"For you died, and your life is hidden with Christ in God" *(Colossians 3:3)*. Christians are to be dead to self—dead to the lure of the world and its decaying force. Our true life is in Christ. We are secure in His love, and because He lives, we will live also.[39]

Don't be afraid of dying to self—there's a better life to be enjoyed! As you pray to surrender to God, take courage in Moses' words, "Stand still, and see the salvation of the Lord, which He will accomplish for you today" *(Exodus 14:13)*.

Step 3—Arise with resurrection power

Ask and keep on asking and it shall be given you. . . .
For everyone who asks and keeps on asking receives. . . .
How much more will your heavenly Father
give the Holy Spirit to those who ask
and continue to ask Him!
(Luke 11:9–13, AMP).

"Do not be alarmed. You seek Jesus of Nazareth, who was crucified. He is risen!" *(Mark 16:6).* The angel's message to the women at the tomb is the message I give you now. Don't be alarmed at the thought of dying to self. Christ didn't stay in the tomb. He's alive! And so, too, will you be more alive than ever!

"That I may know Him and the power of His resurrection, and the fellowship of His sufferings, being conformed to His death" *(Philippians 3:10).* Once we are conformed to His death, we can finally know the power of His resurrection.

"So I say to you, ask, and it will be given to you; seek, and you will find; knock, and it will be opened to you" *(Luke 11:9).* How do we receive resurrected life after we have died daily? It is the Spirit who gives life.[40] We *ask* for the Holy Spirit daily. We earnestly *seek* the Lord to pour out His Spirit on us. We *knock* on the door of God's heart, in acknowledgement of how much we need the Spirit.

The verbs *ask, seek,* and *knock* in Luke, chapter 11, are linear verbs in the Greek language. This means they are a continuous action. We are to ask and keep on asking—seek and keep on seeking—not because we are begging the Lord, but as a result of our constant need.

"Ever be filled *and* stimulated with the [Holy] Spirit" *(Ephesians 5:18, AMP).* Again, in this verse, the Greek form represents a continuous filling. We need to be baptized—immersed—with His Spirit daily.

It is the Spirit's power that causes us to bear the fruit of love, joy, and peace within our hearts; to develop patience, kindness, and goodness toward humankind; and to express faithfulness, humility, and self-control in our walk with the Lord.[41]

Pressing in to His Presence

God pours His love into our hearts by the Holy Spirit,[42] and only those who are led by the Spirit are God's children.[43] The Spirit is our Teacher.[44] Without Him, we cannot understand the things of God.[45] It is through the power of the Holy Spirit that God works in us to will and to act according to His good purposes, and by the Spirit we are sealed for the day of redemption![46]

I could fill volumes of books writing on the ministry of the Holy Spirit, but this will have to suffice for now. I think enough has been said that we can agree—without His power at work within our lives, we are nothing more than sugar ant substitutes for Christians. Our hour of triumph will come when we understand we cannot save ourselves, and we recognize the glory of our salvation belongs to God!

The Spirit of God is given to those who obey Him.[47] Only one Man ever walked this earth who was given the fullness of the Spirit without measure, and that was Christ Jesus,[48] who walked in perfect obedience. The more we obey, the more we are emptied of self, and the greater the measure of His Spirit that will be given unto us!

Our responsibility is simply to surrender to God, and open up our hearts and let the King of glory come in![49] This is the most important supplication that you and I can make in our daily prayers.

The greatest pursuit of the day

Each morning the priests replenished the supply of oil at the golden candlestick. Let us do the same, making earnest supplication for the pure oil of the Holy Spirit as our source to walk in surrender, run with endurance, and be light bearers to the world. Seek God early—this is the greatest pursuit of the day!

The cause of God is crippled in our lives when we lack passionate, personal prayer and knowledge of His promises. Pray for an unquenchable desire to read God's inexhaustible Word. Cry out to God to be sanctified by His Word.[50]

It is by the Word of God and the Holy Spirit that we develop an intimate oneness with God.[51] Contemplation of His love for us should awaken our awe. We cry out "Abba, Father" and, with faith, believe He will hear our supplications and maintain our cause, as each day may require.[52] Faith in His faithfulness is essential to prayer.

Supplication is a time of presenting our personal requests before God. We don't know how to pray as we should, but the Holy Spirit will come to our aid and teach us.[53]

Having pressed in to His presence in supplication, the "King of kings" now holds out His scepter of love and bids us come a little closer. As we hear His command, "Be still, and know that I am God,"[54] we are prepared to stand in His presence.

The revealed will of God should calm our fears. In the next chapter, we will learn how the unveiling of His will for our personal lives will excite our wonder!

1. Exodus 25:40; Numbers 8:4.
2. Exodus 25:31.
3. Exodus 25:32; 37:17.
4. Exodus 37:19, 20.
5. Exodus 26:36, 37.
6. John 8:12; John 1:4.
7. Isaiah 11:1.
8. Isaiah 60:21.
9. Ephesians 2:10.
10. Romans 8:29; 2 Peter 1:3, 4.
11. Malachi 3:3.
12. 1 John 2:20, 27.
13. Revelation 1:4 (see also Isaiah 11:2).
14. Zechariah 12:10.
15. 2 Peter 3:16.
16. Matthew 5:6.
17. Genesis 32:26.
18. Genesis 32:30.
19. Luke 11:3.
20. John 3:5; Romans 8:14.
21. Titus 3:5.
22. John 14:15; John 16:13; 1 Peter 1:2; Romans 8:14; Matthew 15:8.
23. Mark 12:30; Romans 5:5; Galatians 4:6; Matthew 23:27.
24. Ephesians 4:22–24.
25. Exodus 33:18; 34:6, 7.
26. 2 Peter 1:3, 4.
27. Ephesians 3:20; Philippians 2:13.
28. Romans 4:17.

Pressing in to His Presence

29. Isaiah 55:11.
30. Jeremiah 1:12.
31. Genesis 32:26.
32. 1 Kings 19:12.
33. 1 John 2:15–17.
34. James 4:4.
35. Colossians 3:2.
36. John 10:10.
37. 1 Peter 1:4.
38. Luke 9:25.
39. John 14:19.
40. John 6:63.
41. Galatians 5:22, 23; 2 Timothy 1:7.
42. Romans 5:5.
43. Romans 8:14.
44. John 14:26.
45. 1 Corinthians 2:14.
46. Ephesians 4:30.
47. Acts 5:32.
48. John 3:34.
49. Psalm 24:7.
50. John 17:17.
51. 1 Corinthians 6:17.
52. 1 Kings 8:59.
53. Romans 8:26.
54. Psalm 46:10.

ENTER AND BE STILL, PART ONE

CHAPTER 10

Does God still speak to humankind? Of course He does! The Holy Scriptures are the Word of God, and it is through them that God speaks the loudest—to anyone who will listen. Every time we pick up our Bible to read, we can "hear" the echo of our Father's voice.

Perhaps you are thinking, *What about this still, small voice to which you keep referring, Shelley?* I will attempt to answer that question to your satisfaction by offering scriptural evidence of God's divine guidance, as He impresses thoughts upon our minds by His Spirit. You can put your heart at ease. This will not be some bizarre chasing-after-the-wind teaching.[1]

"God spoke to me, and said . . ." At any time I hear someone say these words, a caution flag flaps furiously in my mind, signaling to pay close attention to the report. If it doesn't line up with the Bible and scriptural principles, I know it did not originate from heaven. God will never contradict His Word, which endures forever.[2] The person who receives a message incompatible to Scripture might be hearing a voice, but it is not God's voice. The aberrant announcement spoken to the misguided soul originated either from his or her own desires (not necessarily evil) or from a demonically inspired source.

"God impressed this thought upon my mind by the power of His Holy Spirit." I realize that's what I *should* say when I share something God has spoken to my heart. That phrase puts people more at ease, in comparison to the abbreviated expression "God said to me." But sometimes I forget to clarify for my audience because it has become so natural to accept that God shares His thoughts with me.

Hearing from my heavenly Father does not make me special. It is a privilege of God's children, and I would hope you understand this phenomenon through personal experience.

> The Lord God has given Me the tongue of a disciple and
> of one who is taught, that I should know how to speak
> a word in season to him who is weary. He wakens Me
> morning by morning, *He wakens My ear to hear* as a
> disciple [as one who is taught]. The Lord God has opened
> My ear, and I have not been rebellious or turned backward
> *(Isaiah 50:4, 5, AMP; emphasis added).*

In the prophetic Messianic message of Isaiah 50, the Servant of the Lord proclaims that God "wakens My ear to hear." The ears of Christ were trained to listen for—and anointed to hear—the Father's voice. The purpose of this chapter, and the next, are to teach us the same. As we abide in Christ, we are to walk as He walked.[3]

Allowing Scripture to be our guide, we will briefly look at the various ways God has communicated to His people throughout the ages, with whom He speaks, and what types of messages He delivers. First, let's look at the symbolic significance of the earthly sanctuary's Most Holy Place.

The Most Holy Place

The Most Holy Place was a fifteen foot cube, its length being the same as its width and height. Also called the "Holy of Holies" or "the Holiest," this second compartment was representative of the New Jerusalem, the heavenly city foursquare.[4]

Covering the interior walls and ceiling were magnificent curtains of blue, purple, and scarlet-colored yarn[5] (spun by the women and woven by the men), resplendent with artistic designs of cherubim embroidered in gold and silver threads.[6] The Most Holy Place was a *type* of heaven.

The only piece of furniture within the Most Holy Place was the ark of the covenant. Exquisitely designed, this was the most sacred of all sanctuary objects. To demonstrate its preeminence, the ark was the first article God commanded Moses to make[7] and it was the only thing taken from the original sanctuary into the temple built by Solomon.[8]

The ark of the covenant was the throne of God on earth. This sacred chest contained the two tables of stone upon which God wrote His Ten Commandments with His own finger[9] (these words are the only portion of Scripture hand-recorded by God). The two tables of His commandments represent twin pillars that support the moral foundation upon which God's government rests.

In contrast, the book of the Law (or "Book of the Covenant," the special covenant terms God made with Israel at Mount Sinai, written by Moses' hand), was placed in a pocket on the *outside* of the ark.[10] Its placement was symbolic of the temporary terms of the Old Covenant. As a memorial for God's supernatural provision, a golden pot of manna was placed inside.[11] This was another representation of God's Word as our spiritual nourishment. Also included inside the ark was Aaron's rod that budded (a sign given to verify Aaron had the right to serve as high priest).[12] The rod represented Christ, our Branch[13] who was dead, then resurrected with new life to serve as our only High Priest in heaven.[14]

The ark was covered by the mercy seat,[15] which had two cherubim—one at each of opposite ends.[16] The mercy seat and cherubim were a single piece, fashioned of pure gold. It was here that the visible presence, the Shekinah glory, of God filled the space between the cherubim.[17] Here God communed with people and heard their prayers.

The Holy of Holies was consecrated by the presence of God. The mystic Shekinah (a Hebrew word, not found in the Bible) was seen only by the high priest, who alone could enter the sacred enclosure. All others who heard God's voice from the tabernacle, stood before the golden altar of incense and listened through the veil that separated the Most Holy Place from the first compartment.[18]

"But into the second part the high priest went alone once a year, not without blood, which he offered for himself and for the people's sins committed in ignorance" *(Hebrews 9:7)*. Only on the Day of Atonement did the high priest gain entrance.[19] As he interceded for the people's sins "committed in ignorance,"[20] sprinkling the blood of the sacrifice on the mercy seat, it was there that God extended mercy.

The veil (hanging door) between the two compartments was predominantly blue, symbolic of Christ entering heaven through the blue skies.[21] As our High Priest, He entered—"once for all"[22]—into the true Holy of Holies in heaven. His own precious blood sprinkled on the mercy seat of God is the only thing that provides us forgiveness of sins.

> Therefore, brethren, having boldness to enter the Holiest
> by the blood of Jesus, by *a new and living way* which
> He consecrated for us, through the veil, that is, His flesh,
> and having a High Priest over the house of God,
> let us draw near with a true heart in full assurance of faith
> *(Hebrews 10:19–22; emphasis added).*

At the moment Christ died on the cruel cross of Calvary, the veil in the earthly temple was torn in two—from top to bottom[23]—attesting to the end of the Mosaic sacrificial system. Jesus opened a "new and living way" for us to enter the Most Holy Place with boldness, gaining direct access to our Father's throne of grace.

Let us never take for granted what manner of love has been lavished upon us.[24] As children of God, we share in the privilege of communicating with our Lord heart-to-heart before His very throne. As we enter the Holy of Holies, the holiest place of all, let us remove our casual shoes and enter with reverence—for surely, we are standing on holy ground.[25] Prayer is an awe-inspiring privilege![26]

"Be still, and know that I am God" *(Psalm 46:10).*

"He who has an ear, let him hear what the Spirit says to the churches. To him who overcomes I will give some of the hidden manna to eat" *(Revelation 2:17).*

God is our loving "Abba, Father." When we cry out in supplication, He responds. As a truly perfect Father, He desires to speak words of encouragement, instruction, and even discipline into our hearts. I pray we will learn to train our ears to recognize His authentic voice, and open them to listen. He will give us a taste of His hidden manna to eat, unveiling His will for our lives as we press in to His presence.

Divine means of communication

Let's look at the ways in which the Lord speaks to His people. In the condensed Bible study that follows, I will briefly present ten categories of communication from God.

1. Scripture
2. Prophets and His Son, Christ Jesus
3. Appearances of angels
4. Creation and creatures
5. Answered prayers
6. Signs and circumstances
7. Visions
8. Dreams
9. Audible voice
10. Still, small voice

Scripture

"All Scripture is given by inspiration of God, and is profitable for doctrine, for reproof, for correction, for instruction in righteousness" *(2 Timothy 3:16).*

Clearly, the premier manner in which God speaks to His people is through His Written Word. Through the ages the scrolls and texts of the original manuscripts, now carefully translated into so many languages, have revealed an unfolding of the character of God, His purposes for humankind, and the plans He has for our lives. The Bible remains today the best-selling Book of all time.

"For the Word that God speaks is alive and full of power [making it active, operative, energizing, and effective]" *(Hebrews 4:12, AMP).* "It is in truth, the word of God, which also effectively works in you who believe" *(1 Thessalonians 2:13).* This Holy Book was God-breathed and remains alive and active forever. It contains words—straight from heaven—which have soul-saving transforming power when implanted in our hearts.[27]

Pressing in to His Presence

God speaks through the Bible today. Each time we read His Word, allowing the Holy Spirit to aid our comprehension,[28] His divine counsel echoes in our hearts. Understanding doesn't come all at once.[29] God leads us in baby steps—giving us first the milk of the Word, then the solid food as we are able to digest it.[30] Studying "every word that comes from the mouth of God" and putting His teachings into practice, feeds our spiritual lives and helps us grow to maturity.[31]

Prophets and His Son, Christ Jesus

"God, who at various times and in various ways spoke in time past to the fathers by the prophets, has in these last days spoken to us by His Son, whom He has appointed heir of all things, through whom also He made the worlds" *(Hebrews 1:1, 2)*.

Much of the written texts of the Bible are the recorded words of the prophets and of Christ Jesus. Some mistakenly think there is a variance between the portrayal of God's personality in the Old Testament and the New. They presume the ancient prophets portrayed God as full of wrath, whereas Jesus portrayed Him as the essence of love. What they fail to understand is that our "God of love" raised up prophets to warn a rebellious people of His coming justice if they would not mend their ways.

"Yet for many years You had patience with them, and testified against them by Your Spirit in Your prophets. Yet they would not listen" *(Nehemiah 9:30)*. God is long-suffering with humankind. The desire of His heart is for all to be saved—He takes no pleasure in the death of the wicked.[32] The Old Testament is filled with warnings of impending wrath if the people did not turn back to their heavenly Father. Like a patient parent who gets little joy from punishing a child, God's messages through His prophets often implied, "I'm going to tell you one more time; don't make Me spank you!"

"Knowing this first, that no prophecy of Scripture is of any private interpretation, for prophecy never came by the will of man, but holy men of God spoke as they were moved by the Holy Spirit" *(2 Peter 1:20, 21)*. Prophetic interpretation seems to confuse some who pluck meanings from outside sources to explain symbols of Scripture. The apostle Peter warns against this private interpretation. All symbolic language found in the Bible is explained in the Bible—God doesn't leave interpretation to guesswork. He moved His prophets by the Holy Spirit. They didn't write thoughts of their own.

"It shall come to pass afterward that I will pour out My Spirit on all flesh; your sons and your daughters shall prophesy" *(Joel 2:28; see also Acts 2:17, 18)*. Jesus instituted a fivefold ministry for the equipping of the saints, giving some to be apostles, some prophets, some evangelists, and some pastors and teachers.[33]

"Surely the Lord GOD does nothing, unless He reveals His secret to His servants the prophets" *(Amos 3:7)*. The gift of prophecy is a gift of the Spirit, which continued beyond the days of the early church. But, beware of the false prophets Jesus warns will rise up in the end times![34] Don't be fooled—test the spirits.[35] Does their message line up in agreement with Scripture? You must know the Word of God and the character of the person who claims to be a prophet. Does he or she meet Bible qualifications?

"Do not spurn the gifts and utterances of the prophets [do not depreciate prophetic revelations nor despise inspired instruction or exhortation or warning]. But test and prove all things [until you can recognize] what is good; [to that] hold fast" *(1 Thessalonians 5:20, 21, AMP)*. No prophetic message from God will contradict what He has said in His Word!

" 'Is not my word like fire,' declares the LORD, 'and like a hammer that breaks a rock in pieces? Therefore,' declares the LORD, 'I am against the prophets who steal from one another words supposedly from me. Yes,' declares the LORD, 'I am against the prophets who wag their own tongues and yet declare, "The LORD declares." Indeed, I am against those who prophesy false dreams,' declares the LORD. 'They tell them and lead my people astray with their reckless lies, yet I did not send or appoint them. They do not benefit these people in the least,' declares the LORD" *(Jeremiah 23:29–32, NIV)*.

"Then the LORD answered Job out of the storm. He said: 'Who is this that darkens my counsel with words without knowledge?' " *(Job 38:1, 2, NIV)*. Speaking on behalf of God carries a fearful responsibility. He will not let man put words in His mouth. Pastors, evangelists, teachers, and those who counsel in His name are entrusted with a divine privilege, and are held accountable before the Almighty for what they speak. Most especially is this true for the prophet, who—when representing a declaration from the Lord—must speak only as the Spirit gives utterance.

Does this mean every word the prophet speaks is infallible? No! They are human beings, like you and me, and may speak their own sincere opinion from time to time and yet be sincerely wrong.

A case in point is the story of Nathan the prophet found in 2 Samuel 7. When King David expressed his desire to build a house for God, Nathan said, "Go, do all that is in your heart, for the LORD is with you" *(2 Samuel 7:3)*. Nathan spoke from his own reasoning, for it had been proven to him that God was with David, and surely it seemed a good idea to build God a permanent home on earth. But the "word of the Lord" came to the prophet that night, to alert him that he had spoken in error. It wouldn't be David who built God's temple, but rather his son, Solomon.

Nathan was definitely a prophet chosen by God, but not every word he uttered represented a declaration from the Lord. It is the implication of "Thus saith the Lord . . ." that must be exactly on target. Any message delivered as though it were directly issued from the throne of God must be put to the test.

" 'But the prophet who presumes to speak a word in My name, which I have not commanded him to speak, or who speaks in the name of other gods, that prophet shall die.' And if you say in your heart, 'How shall we know the word which the LORD has not spoken?'—when a prophet speaks in the name of the LORD, if the thing does not happen or come to pass, that is the thing which the LORD has not spoken; the prophet has spoken it presumptuously; you shall not be afraid of him" *(Deuteronomy 18:20–22)*.

"To the law and to the testimony! If they do not speak according to this word, it is because there is no light in them" *(Isaiah 8:20)*. "For the testimony of Jesus is the spirit of prophecy" *(Revelation 19:10)*. The true prophet of God will never speak a word that is not in harmony with the will of God as revealed in the Bible or that does not honor His Living Word, Jesus Christ.

In a Messianic prophecy, God said, "I will raise up for them a Prophet [Jesus] like you from among their brethren, and will put My words in His mouth, and He shall speak to them all that I command Him. And it shall be that whoever will not hear My words, which He speaks in My name, I will require it of him" *(Deuteronomy 18:18, 19)*.

"For since He Whom God has sent speaks the words of God [proclaims God's own message], God does not give Him His Spirit sparingly or by measure, but boundless is the gift God makes of His Spirit!" *(John 3:34, AMP)*. "I assure you, most solemnly I tell you, the Son is able to do nothing of Himself (of His own accord); but He is able to do only what He sees the Father doing, for whatever the Father does is what the Son does in the same way [in His turn]" *(John 5:19, AMP)*.

Even Christ relied on the Spirit to give Him words straight from the throne of God. Every word He spoke was the perfect reflection of His Father's will.

Appearances of angels

"Are they not all ministering spirits sent forth to minister for those who will inherit salvation?" *(Hebrews 1:14)*. One of the many ways in which angels ministered to humankind during Bible days was to deliver messages from God. The prophet Daniel was made to understand visions by the angel Gabriel,[36] who also appeared to Zacharias with news of John the Baptist's birth,[37] and to Mary, announcing she would give birth to the Messiah.[38] Unnamed angels appeared to the women at the tomb,[39] the disciples at Christ's ascension,[40] and the apostle Peter, in his release from prison.[41] This is just to mention a few occurrences.

Does God still speak through angels today? I have no personal experience with this, at least of which I am aware. The Bible advises us to extend hospitality to strangers—for we might be entertaining angels without knowing it.[42] My lack of known angelic encounters does not invalidate this source of ongoing heavenly communication.

A number of sincere-hearted Christians have shared astounding testimonies of what they believed to be an angel's appearance to them. The messages proclaimed were scripturally sound, and the results of heeding the advice brought glory to God, so—as incredible as it seems to me—I accept they were heaven-sent messengers.

Creation and creatures

"The heavens declare the glory of God; and the firmament shows and proclaims His handiwork. Day after day pours forth speech, and night after night shows forth knowledge. There is no speech nor spoken word [from the stars]; their voice is not heard. Yet their voice [in evidence] goes out through all the earth, their sayings to the end of the world" *(Psalm 19:1–4, AMP)*.

Pressing in to His Presence

Many an atheist's heart has been turned to God through the study of astronomy and nature. God is such an artistic Creator and such a genius at organizational systems that His works speak for Him. I personally believe only a willfully blind person can study God's creation and not recognize the eternal power and glory of the Lord.

"What may be known of God is manifest in them, for God has shown it to them. For since the creation of the world His invisible attributes are clearly seen, being understood by the things that are made, even His eternal power and Godhead, so that they are without excuse, because, although they knew God, they did not glorify Him as God, nor were thankful, but became futile in their thoughts, and their foolish hearts were darkened" *(Romans 1:19–21)*.

God speaks through the glory of His creation. Even the workings of an ant or termite colony testify to an intelligent Creator. One incredible Bible report offers an account of the Lord giving human speech to a creature.

Balaam, a false prophet-for-hire of eastern religions[43] (a diviner or conjurer, not a prophet of God), was employed by the king of Moab to curse the Israelites. Against the revealed will of God,[44] Balaam went forth to carry out the deed. The Lord opened the mouth of this false prophet's donkey to speak with the voice of a human to gain his attention.[45] I can't think of a more unusual manner on record in which God has delivered a message of warning.

Answered prayers

" 'Hear me, O LORD, hear me, that this people may know that You are the LORD God, and that You have turned their hearts back to You again.' Then the fire of the LORD fell and consumed the burnt sacrifice, and the wood and the stones and the dust, and it licked up the water that was in the trench. Now when all the people saw it, they fell on their faces; and they said, 'The LORD, He is God! The LORD, He is God!' " *(1 Kings 18:37–39)*.

Elijah prayed earnestly and God answered! His answer was not audible, but Elijah and everyone around him knew God had spoken. When a childless Hannah prayed passionately, God answered by giving her a son, Samuel.[46] After Peter and John were arrested and later released from jail, their fervent prayer, joined with others, brought a remarkable answer.

" 'Now, Lord, look on their threats, and grant to Your servants that with all boldness they may speak Your word, by stretching out Your hand to heal, and that signs and wonders may be done through the name of Your holy Servant Jesus.' And when they had prayed, the place where they were assembled together was shaken; and they were all filled with the Holy Spirit, and they spoke the word of God with boldness" *(Acts 4:29–31).*

God testifies to His nearness and links our hearts to His when He "speaks" to us through answered prayers.

Signs and circumstances

The Angel of the Lord (most Bible expositors agree the "Angel of the Lord" or "Angel of His Presence" is the eternal Word, Jesus Christ)[47] called Gideon to command a group of His people to go up against a vast invading army. An insecure Gideon wanted to make certain it was God who spoke to him.[48]

"If You will save Israel by my hand as You have said—look, I shall put a fleece of wool on the threshing floor; if there is dew on the fleece only, and it is dry on all the ground, then I shall know that You will save Israel by my hand, as You have said" *(Judges 6:36, 37).*

Gideon asked for a sign, and divine grace granted it. The next morning he was able to wring a bowlful of water from the fleece of wool, while the surrounding ground remained bone-dry.[49] Although privileged by a visitation from the Lord, Gideon's faith was still immature. He humbly asked for a second sign (in much the same spirit as Abraham[50] approached God). God allowed and answered the second testing, reversing the sign as Gideon had requested—on the morning after, dew covered the ground but the fleece was dry.[51]

In the next chapter, I will share my "Gideon experience" with you. Just as Gideon questioned whether he was really hearing from the Lord, so did I and asked for a sign. God is so gracious to us who have faith as small as a mustard seed[52]—He causes it to increase! As faith matures, we do not require signs for certainty.

" 'These things says He who is holy, He who is true, *"He . . . who opens and no one shuts, and shuts and no one opens":* I know your works. See, I have set before you an open door, and no one can shut it; for you have a little strength, have kept My word, and have not denied My name' " *(Revelation 3:7, 8; emphasis added).*

When God opens a door for us to do His work, He is communicating His will to us. Paul determined to stay in Ephesus until Pentecost because a "wide door of opportunity" for effectual service was opened to him.[53] In his letter to the Colossians, Paul requested prayer that "God may open . . . a door" for him to speak the Word.[54]

So we see clearly from Scripture that God communicates with His people through circumstances and opportunities.

Visions

" 'And it shall come to pass in the last days, says God, that I will pour out of My Spirit on all flesh; your sons and your daughters shall prophesy, your young men shall see visions, your old men shall dream dreams' " *(Act 2:17).*

When we think of visions from God, we tend to think of prophets such as Daniel or Ezekiel, or the apostle John on the island of Patmos (where he received the vision of the book of Revelation). Yet, the Bible provides reports of believers like you and me who received visions from the Lord.

"Now there was a certain disciple at Damascus named Ananias; and to him the Lord said in a vision, 'Ananias.' And he said, 'Here I am, Lord.' So the Lord said to him, 'Arise and go to the street called Straight, and inquire at the house of Judas for one called Saul of Tarsus, for behold, he is praying. And in a vision he has seen a man named Ananias coming in and putting his hand on him, so that he might receive his sight' " *(Acts 9:10–12).*

God called a little-known disciple, Ananias, to minister to Saul of Tarsus, who had formerly been determined to do Christians harm. At the same time, He gave Saul a vision to receive Ananias as God's representative. Of course, the result was that a murderous Saul experienced both a character and name change, becoming the super-active Spirit-filled apostle Paul. But it wasn't only those God called to special service who received visions.

"About the ninth hour of the day he saw clearly in a vision an angel of God coming in and saying to him, 'Cornelius!' And when he observed him, he was afraid, and said, 'What is it, lord?' So he said to him, 'Your prayers and your alms have come up for a memorial before God. Now send men to Joppa, and send for Simon whose surname is Peter' " *(Acts 10:3–5).*

Cornelius was a pious Gentile, one whose heart searched for God. As a Roman centurion, he had been generous toward the Jewish people. God gave him instructions through a vision to invite the apostle Peter to his home, that he and his household might receive the good news of forgiveness of sins and salvation through Christ.

In the meantime, God had given Peter a vision to prepare his heart for ministry to a Gentile. In vision, Peter saw a great sheet, bound at four corners and filled with unclean animals, and heard the command to rise and eat.[55] Knowing God had forbidden the eating of unclean animals that had not been sanctified by His Word, Peter pondered the symbolic meaning. God provided the interpretation, which Peter shared with Cornelius. "You know how unlawful it is for a Jewish man to keep company with or go to one of another nation. But God has shown me that I should not call any man common or unclean" *(Acts 10:28).*

This serves as a wonderful example of praying to understand any symbolic vision. God will not contradict Himself and will clear any confusion in our minds as we pray to understand His true meaning.

Dreams

When we consider God's messages given through dreams, our minds most likely go to the Old Testament book of Daniel. A pagan king, Nebuchadnezzar, and a prophet of God, Daniel, were given dreams that described the future of world history. Neither man understood the dreams until they were later explained in vision.

Other familiar instances of dreams include Jacob's ladder,[56] the counsel to Joseph to take unto him Mary (the mother-to-be of Jesus) as his wife,[57] and the warning of the wise men from the east to avoid returning to Herod after they found the Christ Child.[58]

God frequently communicated His will to Gentiles through dreams, including pharaoh's chief butler and baker,[59] pharaoh,[60] a Midianite warrior,[61] and Pilate's wife.[62]

At the time of this writing, I am praying for a highly educated man from Mexico whose life was recently turned upside down. He had been devoted to the religious beliefs passed down by of his ancestors until he received a vivid dream from God that called him out of darkness and into His marvelous light. His conversion caused an uproar within his extended family, but the imagery of that dream caused him to become a seeker of truth. His influence on family members to study God's Written Word for themselves has resulted in a number of relatives embracing the same wonderful Bible truths.

Audible voice

"His head and hair were white like wool, as white as snow, and His eyes like a flame of fire; His feet were like fine brass, as if refined in a furnace, and *His voice as the sound of many waters*" *(Revelation 1:14, 15; emphasis added; see also Ezekiel 43:2).*

"The voice of the LORD is *powerful;* the voice of the LORD is *full of majesty*" *(Psalm 29:4; emphasis added).* Any time the Bible mentions the audible voice of the Lord, it is easy to comprehend that it is an awe-inspiring event for humans to hear His voice.

This privilege was granted to Peter, James, and John at the time of Christ's transfiguration. "*We heard this voice* which came from heaven when we were with Him on the holy mountain" *(2 Peter 1:18; emphasis added).* Let's look at the context of this spectacular event.

"Then Peter answered and said to Jesus, 'Lord, it is good for us to be here; if You wish, let us make here three tabernacles: one for You, one for Moses, and one for Elijah.' While he was still speaking, behold, a bright cloud over-shadowed them; and suddenly a voice came out of the cloud, saying, 'This is My beloved Son, in whom I am well pleased. Hear Him!' And when the disciples heard it, they *fell on their faces and were greatly afraid.* But Jesus came and touched them and said, 'Arise, and do not be afraid' " *(Matthew 17:4–7; emphasis added).*

The apostle Paul shared the same privilege and had much the same fearful reaction. "As he journeyed he came near Damascus, and suddenly a light shone around him from heaven. Then he fell to the ground, and heard a voice saying to him, 'Saul, Saul, why are you persecuting Me?' And he said, 'Who are You, Lord?' Then the Lord said, 'I am Jesus, whom you are perse-cuting. It is hard for you to kick against the goads.' So he, *trembling and aston-ished,* said, 'Lord, what do You want me to do?' Then the Lord said to him, 'Arise and go into the city, and you will be told what you must do.' And the men who journeyed with him stood speechless, hearing a voice but seeing no one" *(Acts 9:3–7; emphasis added).*

Can you imagine being at Mount Sinai when the Lord descended upon the mount with fire, and in His majestic and powerful voice spoke to Moses? The Bible record says, "God answered him by voice."[63]

"Now all the people witnessed the thunderings, the lightning flashes, the sound of the trumpet, and the mountain smoking; and when the people saw it, they trembled and stood afar off. Then they said to Moses, 'You speak with us, and we will hear; but let not God speak with us, lest we die' " *(Exodus 20:18, 19).* "Now therefore, why should we die? For this great fire will consume us; if we hear the voice of the LORD our God anymore, then we shall die. For who is there of all flesh who has heard the voice of the living God speaking from the midst of the fire, as we have, and lived?" *(Deuteronomy 5:25, 26).*

It is an awe-inspiring, knee-knocking event to hear the majestic audible voice of the Lord. From Scripture accounts, it would seem it is also a rare event. In the majority of instances today when God's people "hear" His voice, I believe it is the "still, small voice" of the Lord.

Still, small voice

"Then He said, 'Go out, and stand on the mountain before the LORD.' And behold, the LORD passed by, and a great and strong wind tore into the mountains and broke the rocks in pieces before the LORD, but the LORD was not in the wind; and after the wind an earthquake, but the LORD was not in the earthquake; and after the earthquake a fire, but the LORD was not in the fire; and after the fire *a still small voice.* So it was, when Elijah heard it, that he wrapped his face in his mantle and went out and stood in the entrance of the cave. *Suddenly a voice came to him,* and said, 'What are you doing here, Elijah?' " *(1 Kings 19:11–13; emphasis added).*

Although sensational signs accompanied God's message to Elijah, it was, nonetheless, His "still, small voice" that spoke. I have come to understand that when God speaks in this manner, it is the power of His Holy Spirit impressing His thoughts upon our minds.

The apostle Paul was well acquainted with this still, small voice. "And see, now I go bound in the spirit to Jerusalem, not knowing the things that will happen to me there, except that *the Holy Spirit testifies in every city,* saying that chains and tribulations await me" *(Acts 20:22, 23; emphasis added)*.

Philip, one of the first seven deacons of the early church, heard God's still, small voice telling him to go to the Jerusalem-Gaza road, which resulted in the baptism of an Ethiopian treasure. *"Then the Spirit said to Philip,* 'Go near and overtake this chariot.' . . . Then Philip opened his mouth, and beginning at this Scripture, preached Jesus to him" *(Acts 8:29, 35)*.

The book of Acts reports numerous occasions when God impressed His thoughts upon His followers by the "still, small voice" of His Spirit. While Peter meditated on the vision of the sheets and the unclean animals, the Spirit spoke to him.[64] As a group of Antioch believers fasted and prayed, the Spirit spoke saying, "Now separate to Me Barnabas and Saul for the work to which I have called them" *(Acts 13:2)*. At one point, Paul and Timothy were forbidden by the Spirit to preach in Asia.[65] And the prophet Agabus took Paul's belt, bound his own hands and feet, and said, "Thus says the Holy Spirit, 'So shall the Jews at Jerusalem bind the man who owns this belt, and deliver him into the hands of the Gentiles' " *(Acts 21:11)*.

"Now when they bring you to the synagogues and magistrates and authorities, do not worry about how or what you should answer, or what you should say. For the Holy Spirit will teach you in that very hour what you ought to say" *(Luke 12:11, 12)*. How comforting these words from Jesus must have been to His disciples.

I am convinced the Lord continues to impress His thoughts upon the minds of His people through the power of the Holy Spirit. In the past, I didn't understand how to be still before God. He had to break through all of my whirlwind activities to gain my attention. I wonder how many times I ignored His gentle whisper before I allowed Him to train my ears to hear. Forgive me, Lord!

Does God speak today?

"For I am the LORD, I do not change" *(Malachi 3:6)*. "Jesus Christ is the same yesterday, today, and forever" *(Hebrew 13:8)*. Should Christians of this era expect God to speak with them in any or all of these ways? I believe Scripture supports a resounding "Yes" answer (although I don't expect a donkey to speak with me— but then, neither did Balaam). The experience of Christians around the world testifies to the fact that our loving heavenly Father still communicates in an intimate manner with His children today.

"How precious also are Your thoughts to me, O God! How great is the sum of them! If I should count them, they would be more in number than the sand" *(Psalm 139:17, 18)*. In the next chapter, we will consider with whom God speaks and learn how to train our hearts to receive His loving words of encouragement, instruction, and discipline.

"Take heed what you hear. With the same measure you use, it will be measured to you; and to you who hear, more will be given" *(Mark 4:24)*. As we press in to His presence, let us do it with reverence, awe, and a heart filled with expectation. Increase the measure of your expectation—the measure you use will be measured back to you!

---

1. Ecclesiastes 1:14.
2. 1 Peter 1:25.
3. 1 John 2:6.
4. Revelation 21:2, 16.
5. Exodus 35:25; 36:8.
6. Exodus 26:31.
7. Exodus 25:10–22.
8. 1 Kings 8:6.
9. Exodus 31:18; Deuteronomy 10:1–4.
10. Deuteronomy 31:24–26.
11. Exodus 16:33, 34; Hebrews 9:4.
12. Numbers 17:10; Hebrews 9:4.
13. Isaiah 11:1.
14. Hebrews 7:20–28.
15. Exodus 25:17.
16. Exodus 25:18–22.
17. Psalm 80:1.
18. Numbers 7:89; Leviticus 1:1; Judges 20:26–28.
19. Leviticus 16:2.
20. Hebrews 9:7; Leviticus 4:2, 13.
21. Luke 24:50–52; Acts 1:9–11.
22. Hebrews 9:12.
23. Matthew 27:51.
24. 1 John 3:1.
25. Exodus 3:5.
26. Flippant prayers are nothing more than vain babbling.
27. James 1:21.
28. 1 Corinthians 2:14.

29. Mark 4:24, 28.

30. 1 Peter 2:2; Hebrews 5:13, 14.

31. Matthew 4:4; Luke 11:28.

32. 1 Timothy 2:4; Ezekiel 33:10.

33. Ephesians 4:11.

34. Matthew 24:11, 24.

35. 1 John 4:1.

36. Daniel 8:16, 17.

37. Luke 1:18, 19.

38. Luke 1:26–38.

39. Matthew 28:5–7.

40. Acts 1:9–11.

41. Acts 5:19.

42. Hebrews 13:2.

43. Numbers 22:7.

44. Numbers 22:9–12.

45. Numbers 22:22, 23.

46. 1 Samuel 1:27.

47. Genesis 16:11–13; 22:11–17; 24:7; 31:11–13; Exodus 3:2–6; Judges 2:1; 13:13–23.

48. Judges 6:17.

49. Judges 6:36–38.

50. Genesis 18:30, 32.

51. Judges 6:39, 40.

52. Matthew 17:20.

53. 1 Corinthians 16:8, 9.

54. Colossians 4:3.

55. Acts 10:9–17.

56. Genesis 28:12, 13.

57. Matthew 1:20, 21.

58. Matthew 2:12.

59. Genesis 40:5.

60. Genesis 41:1–8.

61. Judges 7:13.

62. Matthew 27:19.

63. Exodus 19:19.

64. Acts 10:19.

65. Acts 16:6.

Enter and Be Still, Part Two

CHAPTER 11

On that September morning of 1999, as God first taught me to *press in* to His presence, I became absorbed in earnest prayer to the One who loves me most. Finally giving myself permission to glance at the clock, I was surprised to see I had spent more than two hours talking to the Lord.

The deep intimacy of that prayer session delighted my soul. Satisfied, I typed the words "In Jesus' name, Amen!" As soon as I added the exclamation point, the Lord added one of His own.

"Be still, and know that I am God!"

This was to be a major turning point in my life.

Stunned by His unexpected command, I stood at a crossroads and tried to trust God's continued leading. Was this really the Lord's voice or merely my own subconscious thought? Doubt, revolving in my mind, ruined my attempts to be still.

"O Lord, is this *You*, or is this *me*?"

Unfamiliar thoughts were impressed upon me. Franticly, I questioned again and again—desperately wanting to identify the source breaking through the silence.

"I will teach you to quit interrupting in the spiritual realm as well as the physical realm. Write what I speak to you that you may take note of it often."

In hindsight, I see the Lord's sense of humor in that remark. Never before had I acknowledged my irritating habit of interrupting others as they spoke, until God pointed out my problem. I believed it was the still, small voice of the Lord.[1] He had my attention and was about to teach me that prayer can be a two-way communication!

Listening for God's gentle whisper during prayer was a novel idea to me. I think perhaps it could be to you, as well. For this reason, in the previous chapter we reviewed the many ways God communicates with the human family. Is He looking for a people who will listen today? Why would the Lord want to impress His thoughts upon our minds by the power of His Spirit?

As we delve deeper into this topic, we will let Scripture guide us to the answers. If we are to entertain this idea of divine communication, it is vitally important to know it is God's will. Equally important, we must learn to recognize His voice— to protect ourselves from following another.

First, let's look at who might expect to hear from God. At the conclusion of our brief review of Scripture, I will share personal experiences of "being still" before God and how life-changing it proved to be.

God communicates with whom?

We have already considered the many ways God communicates with those He calls to be prophets, one of which is to cause them to hear His voice. When God promised to pour out His Spirit on all flesh, one of His stated purposes was to empower His sons and daughters to prophesy[2]—to speak forth His counsel with regard to the future, the present, or even the past. (Not all prophecies are predictions of the future.) God speaks through His prophets to give words of instruction, correction, encouragement, edification (building up of the saints), and comfort.

"For I am the Lord your God. . . . And *I have put My words in your mouth* and have covered you with the shadow of My hand, that I may fix the [new] heavens as a tabernacle and lay the foundations of a [new] earth and say to Zion, You are My people" *(Isaiah 51:15, 16, AMP; emphasis added).*

Whether prophets, kings, disciples, or apostles, *all* the writers of the Bible also heard God's voice—with *spiritual ears,* if not with literal. Every Scripture is God-breathed, given by inspiration of the Lord.[3] God put the "words of His mouth" into His servants' hearts by the power of His Spirit.

"His secret counsel is with the upright" *(Proverbs 3:32).* As a rhetorical question, the Lord asked, "Shall I hide from Abraham what I am doing"?[4] We know from the record, God shared His counsel about Sodom and Gomorrah with upright Abraham. Of course, when we consider God speaking to Abraham, some think of one alarming event and shudder. The story is found in Genesis, chapter 22.

Why would God ask Abraham to sacrifice Isaac, his son of promise—his "seed," through whom the covenant to make him a "father of many nations" would be fulfilled? Did Abraham agonize over his decision to obey the Lord's voice? Did he think it was a cruel test of his faith? I used to believe so, but now understand it differently.

Jesus told the Jews, "Your father Abraham rejoiced to see My day, and he saw it and was glad" *(John 8:56)*. My personal belief is that Abraham saw Christ's day in vision and was comforted at the time God cut covenant with him by animal sacrifice (this story is related in Genesis, chapter 15). Abraham had assurance of God's Calvary plan. He became so familiar with God's voice, that when he was tested to offer up Isaac, the Bible says he went forth in faith, "concluding that God was able to raise him up, even from the dead, from which he also received him in a figurative sense" *(Hebrews 11:19)*. Abraham knew God's Son would be sacrificed and resurrected again. He trusted God to do the same with Isaac.

He takes into His confidence those who are obedient to His will and His Word. The Holy Spirit—given to those who obey[5]—is within us, and leads the children of God by His counsel.[6] He opens our ears to hear as one who is taught by the Lord.[7]

God speaks to those He is trying to turn away from sin. In the previous chapter, we took note of Balaam, who "was rebuked for his iniquity: a dumb donkey speaking with a man's voice restrained the madness of the prophet"[8] and Saul of Tarsus, who—breathing murderous threats against Christians—was knocked to the ground when a light from heaven flashed around him, and he heard the voice of the Lord.[9]

"Therefore, as the Holy Spirit says: '*Today, if you will hear His voice, do not harden your hearts*' "*(Hebrews 3:7, 8; emphasis added)*. I met an old farmer who, after thirty years, still tells his testimony with tears. One moonless and overcast night, this agnostic man was home alone and on a drinking binge. Sometime after midnight, in a blind stupor, he stumbled into his fields and passed out, falling facedown into a trench containing several inches of rainwater. Unconscious, he laid there with his face buried in the mud, under the water. No one knew—but God.

A loud voice roused him, commanding him to "Wake up!" The voice told of His love for this farmer and urged him to repent and mend his ways, that he might receive a second chance at eternal life. The farmer had no doubt it was God's voice he heard. Yielding his heart—and control of his life—to the Lord, he eventually became an active elder in the church.

"The Lord came and stood and called as at other times, Samuel! Samuel! Then Samuel answered, Speak, Lord, for Your servant is listening" *(1 Samuel 3:10, AMP)*. Here we see that God also speaks to those whom He has chosen for a special work. Young Samuel gave God his full attention and permission to speak into his heart—he became a mighty prophet of the Lord. Moses heard the voice of the Lord from a burning bush.[10] Abraham answered the call of God and heard often from the Lord.[11]

Sometimes, the "special" work is not what we expect, as I learned in December 1996. My husband and I had always enjoyed buying gifts for family and friends, particularly at Christmas, when no one was left off our gift list. Still staggering under the weight of the business debt inherited from the "prince"—our infamous Middle Eastern partner—I had been squirreling coins in a can for months to accomplish our holiday shopping. Cashing them in, I was disappointed my stash had amounted to only two hundred dollars.

One Wednesday evening, I returned home from preaching as a guest speaker at a Baptist church. Although I had spoken there before, I didn't know the members all that well. Before I settled in for the night, the Lord impressed me to take money to a couple who had been absent from attendance during that midweek service.

"Yes, Father," I swallowed hard. "How much shall I give them?"

There was no answer. Turning this over in my mind, I approached the Lord with various amounts. Should it be twenty-five? Fifty? A hundred? I was feeling somewhat anxious.

"All of it—give them all you have saved."

"Yes, Lord," I sighed. "I'll take it to them tomorrow."

"Now, child! Take it tonight."

It was after nine o'clock. I had no idea where they lived. They didn't have a phone, so I called several people until I found someone who could provide their address. An hour later, I arrived at their home—the husband answered my knock at the door. Standing outside in the freezing weather, I thrust into his hands an envelope on which I had marked "A gift from the Lord."

"God told me to bring this to you tonight. Don't thank me; thank Him!"

Learning that his wife, Cathy, and their children were ill with the flu, I said a quick prayer and departed. There was joy in my heart, because I knew I had heard from the Lord (it certainly wasn't *my* idea) and had obeyed. On the following Sunday, I ministered at that same church again. Cathy's husband approached me to express his appreciation.

"Boy, was I excited to get that two hundred dollars! I told Cathy we could finally install cable TV!"

The joy of obedience drained momentarily from my heart. Did God direct me to forfeit our Christmas fund for such nonsense? Then the husband shared the rest of the story. The family had awakened the next morning to discover their electricity had been disconnected. It seems they had a haphazard bill-paying habit, and—without realizing it—had fallen three months behind on their payment. Although the weather was bitterly cold, the company refused to restore power until the amount due was paid in full—all $219.20 of it.

Borrowing a neighbor's phone, Cathy pleaded with and cajoled the service representative. She had two hundred. Surely they would carry the balance for a few weeks. Her efforts were in vain—no other option than payment in full would be permitted. Hoping to play on their sympathies, she bundled her sick children and hopped into the car, heading for the downtown office. As Cathy pulled from her driveway, a non-Christian neighbor crossed the street and flagged her down.

Now what? Cathy thought. *She never even speaks to us. What's her problem today?*

"I don't have any idea why I'm doing this, but for some reason I know I am supposed to give you this!" the neighbor snorted.

Tossing something through the car window, she abruptly turned and walked away. A startled Cathy looked at her lap to see what had landed there. It was a twenty-dollar bill! What a testimony she was able to share with the electric company's employees as she paid her bill in full, and held out her hand for eighty cents in change. God had spoken to two somewhat reluctant hearts—one who recognized His voice, and one who didn't—calling them to a special work to keep a poor, sick family from freezing.

When God chose Ananias for a special work, He gave him these words for Saul of Tarsus: "The God of our fathers has chosen you that you should know His will, and see the Just One, and *hear the voice of His mouth*" *(Acts 22:14; emphasis added).* Saul was well schooled in Scripture, a member of the Pharisees, and a student of Gamaliel (a leading rabbinical teacher of his time[12]). Still, he was seriously misdirected and determined to destroy the Christian faith. After his conversion, Saul (Paul) did not consult with other leaders of the early Christian church, but went into Arabia for three years, where he received divine revelation from the Lord and preached the gospel to the Gentiles.[13]

"Everyone who is of the truth *hears My voice*" *(John 18:37; emphasis added).* "The sheep that are My own hear and are listening to My voice; and I know them, and they follow Me" *(John 10:27, AMP).* Our Good Shepherd, Jesus, declared His followers would know and recognize Him.[14] In comparing Himself to a shepherd, He emphatically stated the sheep would know His voice and follow Him only, fleeing from the voice of strangers.[15] As followers of Christ, we become familiar with His voice by studying the Scriptures. Any voice that speaks contrary to God's Written Word will alarm us and send us scurrying in the opposite direction.

God rewards those who earnestly seek Him[16]—people such as King David[17] and Elijah,[18] who ask and *keep on asking,* who seek and *keep on seeking,* who knock and *keep on knocking.*[19] People who perceive God has a good plan for their lives persevere in prayer, seeking Him with all of their hearts.[20] Isaiah was such a man as this. He sought God's face, pressing in to His presence—pressing in to the Most Holy Place, where God was sitting on His throne of grace!

"In the year that King Uzziah died, I saw the Lord sitting on a throne, high and lifted up, and the train of His robe filled the temple. . . . So I said: 'Woe is me, for I am undone! Because I am a man of unclean lips, and I dwell in the midst of a people of unclean lips; for my eyes have seen the King, the LORD of hosts.' Then one of the seraphim flew to me, having in his hand a live coal which he had taken with the tongs from the altar. And he touched my mouth with it, and said: 'Behold, this has touched your lips; your iniquity is taken away, and your sin purged.' Also I heard the voice of the Lord, saying: 'Whom shall I send, and who will go for Us?' Then I said, 'Here am I! Send me' " *(Isaiah 6:1, 5–8)*.

"For the eyes of the LORD run to and fro throughout the whole earth, to show Himself strong on behalf of those whose heart is loyal to Him" *(2 Chronicles 16:9)*. So we see that God is searching to find a people who will listen for His voice.

Let's summarize what we have studied thus far, about how God reveals Himself to us. In the previous chapter, we reviewed ten primary ways in which He communicates with us:

- Scripture
- Prophets and His Son, Christ Jesus
- Appearances of angels
- Creation and creatures
- Answered prayers
- Signs and circumstances
- Visions
- Dreams
- Audible voice
- Still, small voice

In this chapter, we have considered the human classes with whom God speaks.

- Prophets
- Authors of the Bible
- Those obedient to His will and His Word
- Those He is trying to turn away from sin
- Those whom He has chosen for a special work
- Truth-seeking sheep (followers) of Christ
- Those who earnestly seek Him

For accuracy, I must cover two more all-inclusive "classes" of humans who will hear the Lord's voice—those (made righteous by Christ) who will take part in the first resurrection, and those (participators of evil) who are reserved for the second resurrection.[21]

Pressing in to His Presence

"Do not marvel at this; for the hour is coming in which all who are in the graves will hear His voice and come forth—those who have done good, to the resurrection of life, and those who have done evil, to the resurrection of condemnation" *(John 5:28, 29)*. "And many of those who sleep in the dust of the earth shall awake, some to everlasting life, some to shame and everlasting contempt" *(Daniel 12:2)*.

God has a passion for His people and a passion for the lost. The desire of His heart is to communicate His love, light, life, and power to all who will listen and accept His counsel. Some, like stubborn children, stick their fingers in their ears and their tongues out at God, refusing to listen. But the day will come when they hear His voice from their graves.

What the Lord wants us to hear

When we cry out with sincere supplication, the Lord hears and answers. He desires to speak words of encouragement, instruction, and even discipline into our hearts.

> But You, O LORD, are a shield for me,
> My glory and the One who lifts up my head.
> I cried to the LORD with my voice,
> And He heard me from His holy hill
> *(Psalm 3:3, 4)*.

Is your heart breaking right now? God is near to the brokenhearted—He will heal you and bind up your wounds.[22] Are you mourning? Cry out and He will console you—giving you the oil of joy to replace your mourning, the garment of praise to replace the spirit of heaviness.[23]

> He shall call upon Me, and I will answer him;
> I will be with him in trouble;
> I will deliver him and honor him
> *(Psalm 91:15)*.

Blessed be the God and Father of our Lord Jesus Christ, the Father

of mercies and God of all comfort, who comforts us in all our tribulation,
that we may be able to comfort those who are in any trouble,
with the comfort with which we ourselves are comforted by God
(2 Corinthians 1:3, 4).

Do you desperately need direction? Call upon the Lord. Your Teacher will not hide Himself from you. "Your ears shall hear a word behind you, saying, 'This is the way, walk in it,' whenever you turn to the right hand or whenever you turn to the left" *(Isaiah 30:21).*

This is what the LORD says—
your Redeemer, the Holy One of Israel:
"I am the LORD your God,
who teaches you what is best for you,
who directs you in the way you should go"
(Isaiah 48:17, NIV).

" 'Call to Me, and I will answer you, and show you
great and mighty things, which you do not know' "
(Jeremiah 33:3).

God knows the end from the beginning, and He declares things that are not yet done.[24] He confides in those who reverence Him, and causes them to understand His covenant.[25]

How long, O simple ones . . . will you love being simple?
And the scoffers delight in scoffing and [self-confident]
fools hate knowledge? If you will turn (repent)
and give heed to my reproof, behold,
I [Wisdom] will pour out my spirit upon you,
I will make my words known to you
(Proverbs 1:22, 23, AMP).

This reference from Proverbs 1 is the voice of Wisdom calling out. Within the context, Wisdom is personified as a pure and virtuous woman. Whom does Scripture identify as Wisdom? "You have your life in Christ Jesus, Whom God made our Wisdom from God" *(1 Corinthians 1:30, AMP)*. Wisdom lovingly rebukes mockers, desiring to make His heart known to them. God disciplines His children in Wisdom.

"Furthermore, we have had human fathers who corrected us, and we paid them respect. Shall we not much more readily be in subjection to the Father of spirits and live? . . . Now no chastening seems to be joyful for the present, but painful; nevertheless, afterward it yields the peaceable fruit of righteousness to those who have been trained by it" *(Hebrews 12:9–11)*.

> He knows when we need to be lovingly encouraged, and He knows when we need a word of correction.

I am always amused to hear audience responses when I mention I pray for God to discipline me. A collective gasp of horror escapes most lips, as if to imply I was bringing a curse upon my own head. That is as far from the spectrum of God's truth as the color black is from white.

"I will instruct you and teach you in the way you should go; I will guide you with My eye" *(Psalm 32:8)*. God is the perfect Father. He knows when we need to be lovingly encouraged, and He knows when we need a word of correction. If we listen and respond to His gentle words of rebuke, He has to go no further. If we ignore His initial attempts to correct us, He ramps up the volume to gain our attention. Ignore His further pleas, and the consequences of our actions are the punishment.

"Have you not brought this upon yourself by forsaking the Lord your God when He led you in the way? . . . Your own wickedness shall chasten and correct you, and your backslidings and desertion of faith shall reprove you. Know therefore and recognize that this is an evil and bitter thing: [first,] you have forsaken the Lord your God; [second,] you are indifferent to Me and the fear of Me is not in you, says the Lord of hosts" *(Jeremiah 2:17–19, AMP)*.

"And I thought you would call Me My Father and would not turn away from following Me" *(Jeremiah 3:19, AMP)*. Do you detect the note of sadness in our Father's voice here? God wants His children to call on Him by name "Abba, Father."[26] He wants us to trust His leading and His judgment. The longing of our loving Lord is to have children who have ears to hear His voice.[27]

I pray this abbreviated Bible study has increased your awareness that your heavenly Father wants you to listen to His guidance. Hearing from God is not a privilege that belongs to a select few. He wants to train your spiritual ears to hear and recognize His authentic voice. He will never communicate with you in any way that is contradictory to Scripture. With all the commotion of communication in today's chaotic world, it is imperative to know Bible truth so that we can distinguish God's voice above the din, and fine-tune our spiritual antennas to receive only what comes from Him.

> **He wants to train your spiritual ears to hear and recognize His authentic voice.**

Cause me to hear Your lovingkindness in the morning,
For in You do I trust;
Cause me to know the way in which I should walk,
For I lift up my soul to You. . . .

Teach me to do Your will,
For You are my God;
Your Spirit is good.
Lead me in the land of uprightness.
Revive me, O LORD, for Your name's sake!
For Your righteousness' sake bring my soul out of trouble
(Psalm 143:8–11).

As you press in to His presence and reach this final prayer portion, if the idea of "being still" to listen and receive impressions on your heart from God's Spirit makes you too uneasy, I suggest you conclude with a Bible reading to provide opportunity for a divine dialogue, rather than our usual monologue. After all, Scripture is the most significant way we hear from God!

Answering a life-changing call

If I ask you to think of someone who is an artful communicator, you might start considering those who possess eloquent speaking skills. Experts say the most important communication skill anyone can possess is the art of *listening*! If you are not a good listener, then you are a poor communicator—no matter how flowery your speech may be. Some people pray beautiful prayers, but they are so busy talking to God it never occurs to them to listen for His possible response. That was me!

For several years, I had prayed all the Scriptures in this chapter during my practice of affirmations. I thanked the Lord for opening my ears to hear His still, small voice. I thanked Him that I knew and recognized His voice and would not follow the voice of a stranger. But, it never occurred to me to actually try to listen. Yes, God broke through my bustling routine from time to time and impressed His precious thoughts upon my mind. That seemed natural and was all that I expected.

When the Lord taught me to "be still" before Him at the conclusion of my prayer, He changed my life dramatically. For a number of months earlier, I had labored feverishly to develop business-building seminars for our new venture of working with clients of CPAs. We had enough accountants who would promote our services across the United States to fill our seminar pipeline for a year.

With their client-participant estimates of one hundred each, and at a recommended rate of $800 to $1,000 per attendant, the anticipated profit of $50,000 per event (after expenses) dangled before us like a big carrot—not orange in color, but a glimmering karat of gold. I thought surely this was God's answer to clear our debt and make us financially successful.

Developing seminar content had become my all-consuming priority. That is, of course, until God taught me to press in to His presence and showed me He had a greater plan. Although He typically spoke only a few sentences to me each day and often left me with searching questions, it wasn't long before I knew God was calling me into full-time ministry.

My interest in our new business venture evaporated—I was ready to give it up. But the Lord clearly directed that the decision for me to enter full-time ministry must be left up to my husband. God was not discriminating against me as a woman. He knew that J.D. could not launch the company without my help, and we would therefore have to completely abandon our business plans.

This was a time of deep soul-searching for me. Was I sure God was speaking and calling me into full-time labor in His harvest fields? Considering our investment of funds and time in developing our new company, it seemed unlikely that J.D. would be willing to discontinue this business effort—particularly because of the incredible income potential.

"Lord, if J.D. does agree, how can I be certain that we are following Your will? If we decide to do this, would you please give me a sign that we are making the right decision? Would you please do something to confirm our decision, if we make it?"

"This *time I will give you a sign.*"

That's all that was impressed upon my mind, but the message I received was *don't continue to ask for signs.* It seemed God wanted me to learn to trust His leading and keep my eyes on Him rather than seeking signs for proof of His will.

I didn't want to be the one to broach this important topic with J.D., so I asked God to cause my husband to know His will—in His perfect timing. The following weekend, I visited J.D. in the panhandle of Texas where he was working temporarily. As we drove to lunch, I was tempted to open the discussion, but the Holy Spirit reminded me of my request to the Lord. A heavy silence settled over us in the vehicle. Finally, J.D. sighed and asked me a probing question.

"Honey, what's wrong with you? You were so on-fire about our new business, and suddenly you hardly even mention it! Do you even have an interest in it any longer?"

"Yes, I have *some* interest in it," I responded with sing-song insincerity.

"Shelley, if you could do anything in the world, what would you want to be doing?"

"I would be giving Christian seminars to teach people how to have a closer walk with the Lord, rather than giving business seminars to teach people how to be more profitable!" I blurted out my answer without thinking.

God had opened the door for this conversation much sooner than I had expected. My mind and my mouth were racing, as I tried to convey all that had transpired during times of prayer and the heart-change that God had influenced. Still not trusting what God could do in J.D.'s heart, I put forth the idea that perhaps the Lord didn't really mean full time *now*. Maybe I could start in part-time ministry, and we could simultaneously work our new business part time. We could profit plenty to get out of debt and fund the work of the Lord. The ministry could eventually evolve into full time.

J.D. looked uneasy. He had become convinced that I had learned to listen to God's still, small voice, and now he sensed I was holding something back.

"Shelley, you *know* what God is asking you to do, don't you?"

"Yes, I know God is calling me to full-time ministry, and I believe His timing is now."

"Who am I to argue with God?" he answered, without a moment's hesitation.

"Oh, honey, that's wonderful! I asked the Lord to give me a sign, just to make certain that we are making the right decision. So, if this is what we're supposed to do, I'm sure He will confirm it!"

"That's the trouble with *you* Christians—you're always asking for a sign! So, if God doesn't give you a sign soon, does that mean you won't follow His leading into full-time ministry?"

My precious husband was a strong believer in the Lord, and I knew he prayed all the time. He attended church regularly, but in some way he had reserved a part of himself that he wouldn't surrender to God. Sometimes, as now, his faith seemed stronger than mine. I was dumbfounded by his response. What *would* I do if God didn't give me a sign? How long should I wait? How would I even start in full-time ministry? Who was I that anyone would listen to me?

This happened on the first Saturday of January 2000. We determined that afternoon that I would enter into full-time ministry, and our new business pursuit would be shut down. Our decision was made prayerfully and in faith, but with lumps in our throat—not knowing what the future held.

The dew of divine grace

The very next morning I received an unexpected phone call. It was the vice president of an independent Christian broadcasting network that was gaining popularity and coverage in Texas and the surrounding states. She had read my first-edition, self-published book *Life Affirmations From Scripture* and had gone to great lengths to track me down on this weekend—calling various sources to get J.D.'s cell phone. She invited me to come to the studios and tape a program with her.

I felt as giddy as Gideon must have when the dew of divine grace granted him a sign to confirm God's call on his life! I returned to our hometown that night in wide-eyed wonder. Monday morning, as I pressed in to God's presence, the Lord spoke a word of encouragement that would become foundational for my faith in His calling. It is etched in my heart and mind forever.

"Always before you have put your hand to the plow and turned back. But not this time, for I will cup My hand over yours."

It was true, I had *felt* God's call to ministry twice before in my earlier life and had even enrolled in ministerial school. But both times, it seemed as if the gates of hell were opened wide and demonic attacks descended upon my family. Once, I had even angrily shaken my fist at the Lord in response to what happened to my mother and what seemed—at the time—as God's indifference to my earnest pleas on her behalf, and my *forced* faith in His ability to deliver her. That's an odd expression—forced faith. I'm not sure it fits, but I mean to imply that I was under the impression that sufficient faith could force God to act. I had mistakenly developed faith in *faith*, and not faith in *God*.

But now, God's hand was cupped over mine. He had opened a wide door of opportunity for me to minister.

My first television appearance was one I will never forget. Not because of nerves—I was not nervous; I was bursting to share—but because of something the Lord said to me. I had taken extra care to look nice for the cameras, but when I got to the set and glanced at the monitors, I saw my own horrid reflection. The lights were set for the host of the program, who was much shorter than I. Bad lighting cast shadows on my face that made me look ten years older. I was mortified.

"Crucify that thought. This is not about you. It is about Me!"

That's another jewel of wisdom from the Lord to which I constantly cling. It's a great weapon against insecurity about my appearance.

For the next eight months, I appeared regularly on the network. They offered me a series of my own, without production costs or airtime fees. One of their regular paying programmers, a pastor of a huge church, made certain that I understood the great gift God had dropped in my lap—it cost his ministry over $200,000 a year for his weekly program.

The morning I left to start taping the new series, God spoke during my time of prayer and said, *"I am calling you out of where you are."* I thought perhaps we would be relocating to the city where this network headquartered so that I could increase my work there.

That was not God's intent. A misunderstanding over contract terms occurred with the network's general manager during the week while I was taping. I was stunned at the ferocity of his attack against me.

The Lord assured me in prayer, *"The cloud of My presence is moving, and you must follow."* My departure from the network was disappointing, but I left on amicable terms with the precious people who had founded that work.

Following the cloud

God opened other opportunities, and soon I was ministering on a weekly basis in five different cities. Life was pleasant for me, but perplexing for my poor husband. J.D. was not only carrying the full financial load for our personal expenses and debt, but now had to cover the ministry expenses. He was convinced I was following God, but confused about how I heard the Lord's leading.

"I pray throughout the day. Why haven't I ever heard God?" he questioned.

"Well, have you ever been still and listened?"

Several days later, during one of his many daily calls, he cautiously shared a new experience from his prayer time that morning.

"I tried what you said. I prayed—then I listened. I might have heard from God. I'm not sure. How do you know for certain?"

"Well, honey, tell me what was impressed upon your mind," I gently encouraged him.

"The thought I heard was this. 'I am the Potter—you are the clay. I mold you and shape you, then set you on the shelf to cure. But you do not stay settled. You move out of place, always trying to live on the edge. Before you can be made firm, you lean too far in the wrong direction and topple off the shelf. Then, when you cry out, I must pick you up to mold you and shape you again. Move back from the edge!' "

Tears brimmed in my eyes. I *knew* J.D. had heard from God. He was one of the best men I had ever met in my life—compassionate, honest, humble, tenderhearted, but afraid to commit his life fully to the Lord. God had called J.D. to be a pastor when he was younger, and he regretted that he had not responded to His call.

A few weeks later, as I was praying about the future of my own calling, the Lord shared this thought with me.

"I will join you to one who is running fast after Me, and J.D. will work shoulder to shoulder with you and this one." I knew this was God's voice and not my own imagination, because I was somewhat disappointed initially. I'm embarrassed to admit, but I

remember thinking, *I thought You called me to a full-time teaching ministry. I didn't know You wanted me to be another man's assistant.*

That sounds selfish and prideful—because it was. But God soon worked it out of me, and I looked forward to serving in whatever capacity He had planned. I was just excited that J.D. and I would work shoulder to shoulder. God frequently told me He would do a "quick work" in my husband and make him a leader in His church. And, indeed, He did!

One of the Bible-study groups I was leading was women only, in a town about an hour's drive from our home. God had given me a six-part series that I had been sharing in an intensive two-hour weekly study. We were in our fifth week, and I witnessed how rapidly the Lord was changing this group. The metamorphosis in such a short time was as dramatic as watching larvae become butterflies. On the way home, I lamented my own seemingly slow growth.

"Oh, Lord, You are changing them so rapidly. Change me, Father! Change me!"

"Do you not recognize the changes I have wrought in you, child? And you have yet to thank Me!"

That was one of those shut-my-mouth moments. It is true. The Lord often does a work in my heart that I am slow to recognize. By the time I do, I have to pray and ask Him to show me how He accomplished it. I want to recognize and know His workings, to enable me to teach others and to mark the trail so that I can find my way back should I ever slip off His narrow path.

In March 2001, a little over six months after leaving that first television network, I was happily leading home-group studies in surrounding cities. Attendance ranged from twelve to forty people. It was not as far-reaching as television ministry, but I was busy being faithful with the little things to demonstrate that, should God choose to entrust me, I could be faithful over much.[28] One morning, during my time of "being still" before the Lord, He spoke something to my heart that made it leap for joy!

"I will open doors for you to minister in television, radio, and publishing, and you will speak into all *the world."*

Thrilled, I ran downstairs to share God's exciting report with J.D.

"Honey," he said with furrowed brow, "it seems to me that God already did that, and you walked away. How is anyone going to discover you now in this little town of Coleman, Texas, with a population of fifty-one hundred people? You're stuck in the middle of nowhere."

Pressing in to His Presence

"I am a handmaiden of the Lord. Let it be done to me according to His Word," I responded, paraphrasing Luke 1:38.

The Lord performs His purpose

When God first called me into ministry, He clearly instructed me not to promote myself. I was not to seek ministry opportunities. Rather, He would open the doors and I was simply to walk through them. I knew no one needed to "discover" me, as J.D. so put it. God knew where I lived, and He would lead me where He wanted me to minister.

I encountered many rocky places as I plowed God's harvest fields. But when I became discouraged, I never removed my hand from the plow. How could I? God's hand was cupped over mine! Together, we plowed a straight line.

"I will cry to God Most High, Who performs on my behalf and rewards me [Who brings to pass His purposes for me and surely completes them]!" *(Psalm 57:2, AMP).*

Twenty-one months later, J.D. and I arrived at Three Angels Broadcasting Network for my first scheduled appearance.

"Just think about it, honey! Psalm chapter one hundred thirty-nine, verse sixteen, says all the days of our lives were written in God's book before they ever took shape. God already knew we would be here tonight!" I said, bubbling over with enthusiasm.

J.D. was silent for a moment—then softly responded, "Wow, that's a heavy thought!"

It was December 31, 2002. As God had purposed, I spoke into "all the world" with a teaching for their New Year's Eve live broadcast.

After several more appearances on the network, 3ABN offered to produce and air a teaching series of mine, and they published my companion book, *Exalting His Word.* The program aired internationally on their television and radio networks, and I was invited to make a number of additional guest appearances over the next two years. God had fulfilled His promise.

In February 2005, J.D. and I relocated to accept full-time positions at the network's world headquarters. My precious husband went to work in the pastoral department. Now, he walks in absolute surrender to the Lord and is one of the most godly men I know (I would say *the* most godly, if he would let me). The Lord has opened his ears, and J.D. relies on the leading of the Holy Spirit as he goes about his daily work of praying with people and managing 3ABN's pastoral department.

I wonder where we would be if I had refused God's request to press in to His presence. I wonder how we would be investing our lives if we had not learned to listen for God's still, small voice.

"Behold, I stand at the door and knock. If anyone hears My voice and opens the door, I will come in to him" *(Revelation 3:20).*

Your loving Lord is calling to you. Will you listen, and let Him come to you now? Will you be still and know that He is God?

1. 1 Kings 19:12.
2. Joel 2:28; Acts 2:15–18.
3. 2 Timothy 3:16.
4. Genesis 18:17.
5. Acts 5:32.
6. Romans 8:14.
7. Isaiah 50:4, 5.
8. 2 Peter 2:15, 16.
9. Acts 9:1–15; 26:14.
10. Exodus 3:1–4:17.
11. Acts 7:2–4; Hebrews 11:8; Genesis 12–25.
12. Philippians 3:5; Acts 22:3.
13. Galatians 1:16–18.
14. John 10:14.
15. John 10:4, 5.
16. Hebrews 11:6.
17. Psalm 63:1–4.
18. James 5:16–18.
19. Luke 11:9, 10, AMP.
20. Jeremiah 29:11–14.
21. Revelation 20:5, 6.
22. Psalm 34:18; 147:3.
23. Isaiah 61:3.
24. Isaiah 46:10; Romans 4:17.
25. Psalm 25:14.
26. Romans 8:15; Galatians 4:6.
27. Matthew 13:43.
28. Luke 16:10.

SEEK THE LORD AND HIS STRENGTH

AFTERWORD

We have reached the end of this teaching, so I think it would be beneficial to review the various segments of the PRAISE prayer pattern. As we have learned to press in to His presence, we have followed these steps:

Praise
Repentance
Affirmations
Intercession
Supplication
Enter and be still

God corrected my backsliding when He taught me to tarry an hour each day with Him,[1] and He will do the same for you. Perhaps it's impossible for you to pray an hour every day at this stage in your life, but if you will schedule this time even once a week, I promise you will begin to develop a closer relationship with Him. You can use the PRAISE pattern for shorter sessions of prayer, as well. I begin every morning in this manner. I believe God inspired the order of this prayer purposely to follow the divine pattern of His sanctuary.

Though not a requirement, I encourage you to follow God's advice to Habakkuk and try journaling at least once. "I will stand my watch . . . to see what He will say to me. . . . Then the LORD answered me and said: 'Write the vision and make it plain on tablets, that he may run who reads it' " *(Habakkuk 2:1–3).*

"Seek the LORD and His strength; seek His face evermore!" *(Psalm 105:4).* The Lord is good to those who seek Him and wait expectantly for Him.[2] As your Father, God desires a deeper communion with you. Draw near to Him, so that He can draw near to you.[3] He knows your weaknesses, and will exchange His strength for yours.[4]

God is calling His people to develop an intimate relationship with Christ through prayer. Can you hear Him calling your name? He is inviting *you* to press in to His presence that you may know Him and the plan He has for your life!

I know He will show you the path of life, and you will find fullness of joy in His presence.[5] May the grace of our Lord Jesus Christ, the love of God, and the communion of the Holy Spirit be with you always![6]

---

1. Matthew 26:40.
2. Lamentations 3:25.
3. James 4:8.
4. Isaiah 40:31; 2 Corinthians 12:9.
5. Psalm 16:11.
6. 2 Corinthians 13:14.

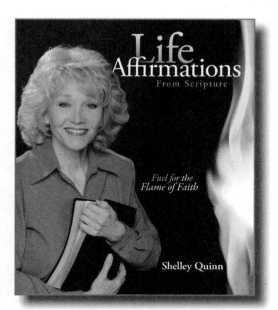

Life Affirmations
From Scripture

Fuel for the flame of faith . . . Want a more dynamic Christian life? Want to get rid of negative self-talk? Are you looking for more faith, hope, and love? Begin here—with the Word of God and this collection of spiritual affirmations that you can speak out loud. Beginning with a prayer and following with texts to read aloud, you will discover the life-changing power of affirming God's Word.

Paperback, 176 Pages
ISBN 13: 978-0-8163-2278-7
ISBN 10: 0-8163-2278-3

EXALTING HIS WORD

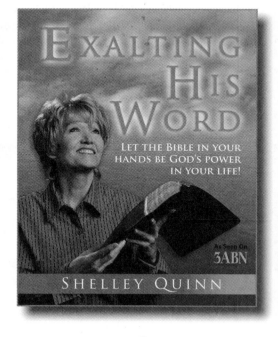

To all who long to know God's plan of love. To all who want a more intimate relationship with God. To all who look for an abundant life and power to walk in Christ's footsteps . . . look no further than the Bible in your hands. If your heart's desire is to break free from the "three-steps-forward, two-steps-back" routine, and to finally experience God's transforming power in your life, it's time to start *exalting His Word!*

Paperback, 176 Pages
ISBN 13: 978-0-8163-2147-6
ISBN 10: 0-8163-2147-7

Pacific Press®
Publishing Association
"Where the Word is Life"